THE POWER
OF THE POWERLESS

The Power of the Powerless

by

CHRISTOPHER DE VINCK

Doubleday

NEW YORK

1988

Acknowledgments

The author wishes to thank the following for permission to quote from previously published material:

Harcourt Brace Jovanovich, Inc. for *The People, Yes* by Carl Sandburg, copyright © 1936 by Harcourt Brace Jovanovich, Inc. and renewed in 1964 by Carl Sandburg. Reprinted by permission of the publisher.

Harper & Row, Publisher, Inc. for excerpts from *The Bridge of San Luis Rey* by Thornton Wilder, copyright © 1927 by Albert and Charles Boni and renewed in 1955 by Thornton Wilder. Reprinted by permission of the publisher.

New Directions Publishing Corporation for excerpts from *New Seeds of Contemplation* by Thomas Merton, copyright © 1961 by the Abbey of Gethsemani, Inc. Reprinted by permission of the publisher.

Charles Scribner's Sons for excerpts from *Look Homeward, Angel* by Thomas Wolfe, copyright © 1929 by Charles Scribner's Sons and renewed in 1957 by Edward C. Aswell, Administrator, C.T.A. and/or Fred W. Wolfe. Reprinted by permission of the publisher.

The John Day Company for excerpts from *The Child Who Never Grew* by Pearl Buck, copyright © 1950. Reprinted by permission of the publisher and The Training School at Vineland, N.J.

Sign magazine for excerpts from *Oliver* by Catherine de Vinck, July, 1977, copyright © by the Passionist Fathers. Reprinted by permission of Fr. Sebastian Kolinovsky, C.P., Procurator, Passionist Missions, Union City, N.J.

Charles Scribner's Sons for excerpts from *The Great Gatsby* by F. Scott Fitzgerald, copyright © 1925 Charles Scribner's Sons; copyright renewed 1953 Frances Scott Fitzgerald Lanahan. Reprinted with the permission of Charles Scribner's Sons.

Library of Congress Cataloging in Publication Data
De Vinck, Christopher, 1951–
The power of the powerless/by Christopher de Vinck.
    p. cm.
ISBN 0-385-24138-0
    1. Catholics—United States—Biography. 2. De Vinck family.
3. Handicapped—Family relationships. 4. Handicapped—Religious
life. 5. Suffering—Religious aspects—Christianity. I. Title.
BX4651.2.D38   1988
248.8′6′0924—dc19
[B]   87-19838
                                                                CIP

To My Parents Catherine and José

CONTENTS

ACKNOWLEDGMENTS

I would like to thank Fred Rogers, Bill Isler and Family Communications in Pittsburgh, Father John Catoir and the Christophers in New York City.

I would like to thank Sargent Shriver, Eunice Kennedy-Shriver, Dr. George Zitnay and the Joseph P. Kennedy, Jr. Foundation in Washington, D.C., Tim Ferguson, Barbara Phillips, John Fund and *The Wall Street Journal,* and I would like to thank Tom Lashnits, Diana Schneider and the *Reader's Digest,* and Dorothy Robinowitz and the New York *Post,* all people and institutions who gave me friendship, confidence and trust, and who all believed, deeply, in my brother's worthiness.

Finally I would like to thank my editor Robert Heller, Father Henri Nouwen, my brothers and sisters, the Holy Spirit, my teacher Donald Ryan at Northern Highlands Regional High School in Allendale, New Jersey, my children David, Karen and Michael, and I would like to thank, and embrace, my wife, Roe.

"Man has survived through tenderness."

Loren Eiseley

FAMILY PORTRAIT

I am no father to a single child
Nor husband to my wife alone,
Nor she mother to her children
Made in curious hours spent
Upon a hidden creation.

No, we are not single in our living,
But part of this ritual dance
Hand in hand, this family.

We embrace beyond the neighborhood
Of ourselves and reach out
To a peculiar root hold.

We can decide to make choices.
What man is born without a voice?
"Love is stronger than death,"
So the wise men say.

Let us choose to discuss the
Secret yearnings in our single house
Built for our singing, this earth
To walk upon with stars to keep
Above our heads.

From door to door, from season
To season, we are the family of hope
Relatives to a greater heritage.

INTRODUCTION
Henri J. M. Nouwen

A few years ago Christopher de Vinck came to visit me for a few days. At that time I was teaching at Harvard Divinity School. I will never forget that visit because Chris was a visitor quite different from most. I was used to receiving people who wanted to share their struggle, who were looking for advice in a project, who were trying to find a publisher for their writing, or who hoped that I could participate in a seminar, a conference or a workshop. But Chris was not that kind of visitor. As soon as he entered the house, I and my friends who were there experienced something refreshingly new. Chris had no great questions, problems or plans. He just came to tell us how beautiful life is, in case we had forgotten. He was so light, sunny, open, uncomplicated and in love that it seemed as if he came from another world. While we had become used to agonizing about the meaning of friendship, the struggles of marriage and the single life, the wisdom of having children, the depressing state of the economy, the endless conflicts in Central America and the Middle East and the threat of a nuclear war, Chris seemed to step beyond all of that and say, "Look how beautiful life is!" He didn't say it so much with words as with his whole presence. He was so radiant, so simple, so transparent that I felt embarrassed by my own and my friends' seriousness. He seemed like a messenger of good news, stepping into my world from another orbit. He spoke mostly about love—love for his parents, his wife, his three children, his poetry, his high school students, his friends and all that is created. His heart was so full of love that he seemed unable to say anything hostile about anybody. Whatever I said or did, he was able to say something good about it, even while I was doubtful, anxious or confused.

As he stayed with me I started to think about him as Nathanael whom Jesus called a man "in whom there is no deception." When he left I had that strange feeling of having "been visited" by an angel of God.

All of this may sound very sentimental and a longer stay of Chris de Vinck might have made me more aware of his shadows. But he did not stay longer and what I saw and felt was very real. I had become aware of a way of seeing the world that I had not experienced for a long time. Chris' eyes and ears were seeing and hearing what many people do not see and hear.

When I read *The Power of the Powerless* in which he tells the story of his brother Oliver and the stories of Lauren, Anthony and Paul, I immediately recognized that only Chris could have written it. It is so full of wonderment, amazement, gratitude, joy, peace and renewal of life that nobody but a person with a special eye and a special ear could have written it.

Because about whom does Chris write? He writes about four very handicapped people, people who suffered from several physical and mental deformations, people who by many are considered misfits, vegetables, tragic flaws of nature, people about whom many feel that it would have been better if they had not been born. But for Chris these people are God's messengers, they are the divine instruments of God's healing presence, they are the ones who bring truth to a society full of lies, light into the darkness and life into a death-oriented world. Everything this book reveals seems contrary to common sense. How can a young man who cannot see, walk, talk, feed himself or communicate in any way and who is on his back in his bed until he dies at the age of thirty—how can such a person be the most life-giving presence in the family? But that is how Chris saw his own brother Oliver and that too is how Chris came to see the lives of Lauren, Anthony and Paul whose families he visited.

The Power of the Powerless breaks with all human logic, all intelligent predictions, all normal norms of success and satisfaction. It turns everything upside down. It speaks not only about the power of the powerless, but also about love offered by those who cannot speak words of love, joy created by those who suffer grievously, hope given by those whose lives are complete failures, courage enkindled by those who cannot make the slightest move on their own. In a world that so much wants to control life and decides what is good, healthy, important, valuable and worthwhile, this book makes the shocking observation that what is hidden from "the learned and the clever" is revealed to "mere children." (Matt. 11:25) Chris summarizes it all when he writes, "If Oliver had never been born, I wouldn't have the same joys and fears and secrets I dream about today. There was a substance in the house of Oliver beyond science and philosophy and theology, for these are man-made explanations. We always feel a need to explain, to touch and hold evidence. We always feel confident that we can make decisions in the present which will guarantee comfortable results in the future. Those guarantees never exist, unless the choices we make embrace the fire in an act of love." (Chapter 15, p. 133) That, too, was the final discovery of those who lived with and loved Lauren, Anthony and Paul.

When I finished reading *The Power of the Powerless* I had a strange vision. I saw our crazy world, full of wars and conflicts, full of competition and ambition, full of heroes and stars, full of success stories, horror stories, love stories and death stories, full of newspapers, television, radios and computer screens, and millions of people believing that something was happening that they couldn't miss without losing out on life. And then I saw a hand moving this heavy curtain of spectacles away and pointing to a handicapped child, a poor beggar, a chronically ill woman, an illiterate monk, a dying old man, a hungry child. I had not noticed them before. They seemed hidden so far away from where "it" seemed to be happening. But the hand pointed gently to these poor, humble, weak people and a voice said, "Because of them I won't let this world be destroyed. They are my favored ones and with them I made my covenant and I will be faithful to it."

When Chris de Vinck visited me I was at Harvard Divinity School. Now, two years later, I am living in one of the L'Arche communities where mentally handicapped people and their assistants try to live together in the spirit of the beatitudes. During Chris' visit I didn't know that I would so soon live with those about whom Chris writes in his book. L'Arche has become my new home, and the mentally handicapped people my daily companions. Every day I spend time with Adam, a twenty-five-year-old man who is as severely handicapped as Oliver. I love him and I know that he loves me, even though there are no words or gestures to express it. It is not an easy life, it is not a comfortable life, but it is an upside-down life that makes me marvel every day about the beauty of the wounded human heart. The Adams and Olivers of this world keep us safe. They keep us sane. They keep this world together. I know it sounds crazy, but I also know that it is true. The truth shall set me free. I am still struggling. Something in me keeps pulling me back to the place of success and praise, the place of newspapers, radios and televisions. It is hard at times to see and hear the event which is right in front of you, the event of true love.

But Chris knew about it all along. His brother had opened his eyes and ears. His book gives me courage to continue on the road I have chosen. May many people who read this book catch a glimpse of what Chris saw. I am sure that—if they do—their lives will be different.

THE POWER
OF THE POWERLESS

Chapter I

A few days after my brother Oliver died, my mother gave me his red dinner bowl. It is blood red, made from thick, inexpensive ceramic.

One Christmas my father received rich plum pudding inside this bowl. He soon discovered that it was just the right size for an egg, cereal, milk, a banana and sugar: Oliver's dinner. So for years and years, during his quiet life, Oliver received all his food from our hands to his lips, that food brought from the kitchen, through the dining room, up the stairs, carried to his room in the red ceramic bowl, the Christmas pudding bowl.

Oliver is buried at the Benedictine Monastery in Weston, Vermont, and his dinner bowl sits on my shelf next to my books in this room where I write.

How often do we reduce the memory of those we love to objects? Photographs. Letters. Tombstones. The spirit of a dead father or mother, the shadows and sounds of a dead sister or brother linger. Often, what is left behind surprises: grief, anger, longing, but then something else, which surprises even more: a new order perhaps, an acceptance, a feeling about things.

I remember when I was seven there came to me a sudden idea which I could not explain except to cry in the darkness of my room. My bed was against the wall. The cars which passed through the night pressed their lights through my window, creating the same pattern of curtain and shade over and over upon the wall. That is the place where I understood for the first time that my mother and father would someday die. That is the end of innocence. It never occurred to me that I would die, but I was aware of a presence, a movement which leans against us. Was it good, or bad? If my mother and father were going to die, well then that was bad, but there was always something else mixed in with the darkness which I did not understand when I was seven, something that I now see which filled Oliver's red dinner bowl each night, something that is somehow linked to the tombstones and old photographs in the boxes we keep.

So much depends upon how we choose to see things and events. We go to Rome to admire the ancient ruins. We go to Auschwitz to kiss the ground in agony and in humble offering of prayer. Guernica, Hiroshima, Chile. We find in the hearts of all countries the occasion of death in all its violence, death in all its routine. We find in the hearts of all men and women the occasion of death, and how we choose to see this event defines life.

I think of Oliver's crooked bones neatly laid together in his coffin deep in the ground of Vermont. Is that bad?

"The more we persist," wrote Thomas Merton, "in the misunderstanding of the phenomenon of life, the more we analyze it out into strange finalities and complex purposes of our own, the more we involve ourselves in sadness, absurdity and despair."

We have buried our dead in wooden boxes and granite sarcophagi. We have suspended their bodies on platforms in trees to dry and wither to dust. Pyramids, catacombs, the pyre. The burial at sea. Ashes scattered.

We celebrate the phenomenon of death admirably, I think. "No more to build on there," Robert Frost laments in his poem "Out, Out—."

What worries me is the building up, the laying of one cell upon another, that constant division upon itself. What worries me is the phenomenon of life: the very first moment we *choose* to give the life growing in us a human name.

There is a strain upon the heart of our country today which has caused much grief. That strain has created a mask we wear and a blindness. Only in the moments of compassion do we, again, recognize the contours of our face and regain our vision.

We are sacrificing the nobility of suffering to the immediate gods of pleasure. We are leaning toward the arrogance of our present comforts, and reeling away from the slightest hindrance to our genteel lives.

In her slim book, *The Child Who Never Grew*, a book about her severely disabled daughter, Pearl Buck wrote, "There must be acceptance and the knowledge that sorrow fully accepted brings its own gifts. For there is an alchemy in sorrow. It can be transmuted into wisdom, which, if it does not bring joy, can yet bring happiness."

One spring afternoon my five-year-old son, David, and I were planting raspberry bushes along the side of the garage. He liked to bring the hose and spray the freshly covered roots and drooping leaves.

A neighbor joined us for a few moments and there we stood, my son David, the neighbor and I. We probably discussed how much water a raspberry plant could possibly endure when David placed the hose down and pointed to the ground. "Look, Daddy!"

If a wasp enters the house, I show my three children, David, Karen and Michael, how I catch the insect with a glass and a piece of thick paper. I wait for the wasp to stop its frantic thumping and buzzing against the windowpane, then I place the open drinking glass over the creature and trap it. Then, without pinching the wasp, I slowly slide the thick paper under the glass, and there I have it.

I invite the children to take a close look. They like to see the wasp's thin wings; then all four of us leave the house through the front door for the release.

The children, standing back a little, like to watch as I remove the paper from the top of the glass. They like to watch the rescued wasp slowly walk to the rim of the glass, extend its wings, and fly off into the garden. We all clap, David, Karen, Michael and I.

When David was two he climbed to the top of the small blue slide one afternoon in our backyard, and just before he zoomed down, he saw a few ants crawling around on the smooth metal. "Daddy! Ants!"

We stopped and crouched down to see if we could count how many legs ants have (six); then I gently brushed the ants off the slide and David shot down with glee.

I choose to catch the wasp and count the legs of an ant.

"Look, Daddy! What's that?" I stopped talking with my neighbor and looked down.

"A beetle," I said.

David was impressed and pleased with the discovery of this fancy, colorful creature.

My neighbor lifted his foot and stepped on the insect giving his shoe an extra twist in the dirt.

"That ought to do it," he laughed.

David looked up at me, waiting for an explanation, a reason. I did not wish to embarrass my neighbor, but then David turned, picked up the hose and continued spraying the raspberries.

That night, just before I turned off the lights in his bedroom, David whispered, "I liked that beetle, Daddy."

"I did too," I whispered back.

We have the power to choose.

Chapter II

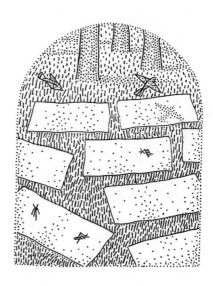

In the winter of 1985, Tom Lashnits of the *Reader's Digest* invited me to Pleasantville, New York, for a luncheon. We were to be joined by another editor, Diana Schneider.

"We would like you to present us with a few article ideas you think we might be interested in."

The *Digest* had reprinted an article of mine a few months before which led to the invitation. It was the first time anyone had taken me to a business lunch.

"Well, I'd like to write an article about the New York bishop, John O'Connor. I could do a piece on an old, old family friend, photographer Nell Dorr. You might be interested in a piece about my good friend Fred Rogers or Henri Nouwen. I could write a piece about my high school English teaching, or about the importance of reading. How about an article on poetry in America?"

The last thing on my list, "I could also write about my brother, Oliver."

The two editors looked at me, drank, ate, listened, then Tom said, "Tell us about Oliver."

"Well, I grew up in a house where my brother was on his back in bed for thirty-two years, in the same corner of his room, under the same window, beside the same yellow walls. He was blind, mute. His legs were twisted. He didn't have the strength to lift his head or the intelligence to learn anything."

The editors sat across the table from me and listened for two hours as I told the story of my brother in all his helplessness, the years of convulsions, the times my brothers and sisters and I tickled his chest and changed his diapers, tended to his meals. I felt like Scheherazade letting words and memories carry a story to the two good people sitting before me.

"That is the article we'd like you to write. We would be interested in Oliver."

Lunch was over.

This is wonderful, I thought as I drove home. That winter night I wrote and wrote, remembering the color of Oliver's bedroom, the sound of his cough. I sat at my desk and thought about Helen Keller. I thought about Pearl Buck, Loren Eiseley, Oliver's baptism certificate. I thought about my mother and father, my brothers and sisters.

I wrote for two or three weeks between my high school teaching, between changing the diapers of our children, and between embracing my wife.

I remembered Oliver's husky laugh, the grasshoppers on the diapers and sheets my mother spread out upon the lawn to dry so many years ago. I wrote and I wrote, remembering the sun, Oliver's last breath, and I remembered the red bowl.

I discovered, although Oliver had been dead for five years, how much still lingered which I plucked like fruit to be eaten.

After one draft, after a second, a third, and after a fourth this, simply, is the essay I wrote which changed my life and the lives of so many people who read it:

I grew up in the house where my brother was on his back in his bed for thirty-two years, in the same corner of his room, under the same window, beside the same yellow walls. He was blind, mute. His legs were twisted. He didn't have the strength to lift his head or the intelligence to learn anything.

Oliver was born with severe brain damage which left him and his body in a permanent state of helplessness.

Today I am an English teacher, and each time I introduce my class to the play about Helen Keller, The Miracle Worker, *I tell my students the story about Oliver.*

One day, during my first year of teaching, I was trying to describe Oliver's lack of response, how he had been spoon-fed every morsel he ever ate, how he never spoke. A boy in the last row raised his hand and said, "Oh, Mr. de Vinck. You mean he was a vegetable."

I stammered for a few seconds. My family and I fed Oliver. We changed his diapers, hung his clothes and bed linens on the basement line in winter, and spread them out white and clean to dry on the lawn in the summer. I always liked to watch the grasshoppers jump on the pillowcases.

We bathed Oliver, tickled his chest to make him laugh. Sometimes we left the radio on in his room. We pulled the shade down on the window over his bed in the morning to keep the sun from burning his tender skin. We listened to him laugh as we watched television downstairs. We listened to him rock his arms up and down to make the bed squeak. We listened to him cough in the middle of the night.

"Well, I guess you could call him a vegetable. I called him Oliver, my brother. You would have loved him."

One October day in 1946, while my mother was pregnant with Oliver, her second son, my father rose from bed, shaved, dressed, and went to work. At the train station he realized he had forgotten something, so he returned to the house and discovered the smell of gas leaking from the coal-burning stove.

My mother was unconscious in her bed. My oldest brother was sleeping in his crib which was quite high off the ground so the gas did not affect him. My father pulled them out of the room, through the hall, and outside where my mother revived quickly. And that was that.

Six months later, on April 20, 1947, Oliver was born. A healthy-looking, plump, beautiful boy.

"Oliver seemed like any other newborn," my mother and father told my sisters and brothers and me over the years, as they repeated the story with their deep love and joy. "There was no sign that anything was amiss."

One afternoon, a few months after he was born, my mother brought Oliver to a window. She held him there in the sun, the bright good sun, and there Oliver rested in his mother's arms, and there Oliver looked and looked directly into the sunlight, which was the first moment my mother realized that Oliver was blind.

My parents, the true heroes of this story, learned with the passing months that Oliver could not hold up his head, could not crawl, walk, sing; he could not hold anything in his hand; he could not speak. So they brought him to Mt. Sinai Hospital in New York City for a full series of tests to determine the extent of his condition.

The only explanation anyone could agree upon was that the gas which my mother inhaled in her sleep during the third month of her pregnancy had reached Oliver and caused the severe, incurable, hopeless condition before he was born.

At the end of a long week of waiting, my parents returned to the hospital and met with the doctor, Dr. Samuel De Lange.

When our children are in pain, we try to heal them. When they are hungry we feed them. When they are lonely we comfort them.

"What can we do for our son?" my parents wanted to know.

Dr. De Lange said that he wanted to make it very clear to both my mother and father that there was absolutely nothing that could be done for Oliver. He didn't want my parents to grasp at false hope.

"You could place him in an institution."

"But," my parents answered, "he is our son. We will take Oliver home, of course."

The good doctor said, "Then take him home and love him." That was sound medical advice.

Dr. De Lange speculated that Oliver would probably not live beyond the age of seven or eight; he also suggested that Oliver be taken to another neurosurgeon to confirm the diagnosis. This is what my parents did and, yes, the second doctor repeated the first verdict. Oliver's case was hopeless.

While he scanned the forms my parents filled out, the second doctor noticed that both my mother and father were born in Brussels, which led the doctor to say, "During World War II my parents were taken in, fed and protected by a Belgian family for we are Jews. Now it is my turn to help a Belgian family," and the doctor didn't charge my parents for all the tests, the care and medication.

I never met these two doctors, but I loved them all my life as a child loves the heroes in a fairy tale.

Oliver grew to the size of a ten-year-old. He had a big chest, a large head. His hands and feet were those of a five-year-old, small and soft. We'd wrap a box of baby cereal for him at Christmas and place it under the tree. We'd pat his head with a damp cloth in the middle of a July heat wave. His baptismal certificate hung on the wall above his head. A bishop came to the house and confirmed him.

Oliver still remains the most hopeless human being I ever met, the weakest human being I ever met, and yet he was one of the most powerful human beings I ever met.

As a teacher, I spend many hours preparing my lessons, hoping that I can influence my students in small, significant ways. Thousands of books are printed each year with the hope that the authors can move people to action. We all labor at the task of raising our children, teaching them values, hoping something "gets through" to them after all our efforts.

Oliver could do absolutely nothing except breathe, sleep, eat, and yet he was responsible for action, love, courage, insight.

For me, to have been brought up in a house where a tragedy was turned into a joy, explains to a great degree why I am the type of husband, father, writer and teacher I have become.

I remember my mother saying when I was small, "Isn't it wonderful that you can see?" And once she said, "When you go to heaven, Oliver will run to you, embrace you, and the first thing he will say is 'Thank you.' " That leaves an impression on a boy.

Of course it is I who must thank Oliver and my parents for defining for me the boundaries of love which were the house, the yard, the woods where my sisters and brothers and I ran in and out all day long, the fields where we ice-skated in the winter and caught snapping turtles in the summer, and all the time Oliver laughed and slept between his fresh sheets, under the window day after day.

I remember, too, my mother explaining to me that we were blessed with Oliver in ways that were not clear to her at first.

We were fortunate that Oliver's case was so severe. The best we could do for him was feed him three times a day, bathe him, and keep him warm. He did not need us to be there in the room all day. He never knew what his condition was. We were blessed with his presence, a true presence of peace.

So often parents are faced with a child who is severely re-

tarded, but who is also hyperactive, demanding or wild, who
needs constant care. So many people have little choice but to
place their child in an institution. Each circumstance is different.
No one can judge.

I have come to believe we are here to tend to the lilies of the
field. We do the best we can. If you have a boy or girl like Oliver
in your home, you will know what is best for him or her, for your
family. The decision is never easy.

I asked my father, "How did you care for Oliver for thirty-two
years?"

"It was not thirty-two years," he said. "I just asked myself,
'Can I feed Oliver today?' and the answer was always, 'Yes I
can.'"

We lived with Oliver moment by moment.

I remember once when I was a little boy sitting down beside
my brother. I was alone in the house, and I wanted to see if Oliver
was really blind, if he was faking it, so I spread my right hand
over his face and shook my fingers close to his open eyes. Of
course he did not blink, did not move. His eyes were brown, like
mine, yet so different.

Often it was my job to feed Oliver supper: a poached egg mixed
with cereal, warm milk, sugar, a banana. Yuck, I often thought. I
wouldn't eat this stuff.

Feeding Oliver throughout his life was like feeding an eight-
month-old child. His head was always propped up to a slight
incline on pillows. A teaspoon of food was brought to his lips. He
would feel the spoon, open his mouth, close his mouth, and
swallow. I still, today, can hear the sound of the spoon ticking
and tapping against his red bowl in the silence of his room.

"Oh, Mr. de Vinck. You mean he was a vegetable."

When I was a child I was afraid of the dark and shared a room
with my younger brother. Our room was separated from Oliver's
room by a single wall. Five inches of wood and plaster divided us
from each other during the night. We breathed the same night air

as Oliver did, listened to the same wind, and slowly, without our knowing, Oliver created a certain power around us which changed all our lives. I cannot explain Oliver's influence except to say that the powerless in our world do *hold great power. The weak* do *confound the mighty.*

When I was in my early twenties I met a girl and I fell in love. After a few months I brought her home for dinner to meet my family.

After the introductions, the small talk, my mother went to the kitchen to check the meal, and I asked the girl, "Would you like to see Oliver?" for I had, of course, told her about my brother.

"No," she answered. She did not want to see him. It was as if she slapped me in the face, yet I just said something polite and walked to the dining room.

Soon after, I met Roe, Rosemary, a dark-haired, dark-eyed, lovely girl. She asked me the names of my brothers and sisters. She bought me a copy of The Little Prince. *She loved children. I thought she was wonderful.*

I brought her home after a few months to meet my family. The introductions. The small talk. We ate dinner; then it was time for me to feed Oliver.

I walked into the kitchen, reached for the red bowl and the egg and the cereal and the milk and the banana and prepared Oliver's meal. Then, I remember, I sheepishly asked Roe if she'd like to come upstairs and see Oliver. "Sure," she said, and up the stairs we went.

I sat at Oliver's bedside as Roe stood and watched over my shoulder. I gave him his first spoonful, his second. "Can I do that?" Roe asked. "Can I do that?" she asked with ease, with freedom, with compassion, so I gave her the bowl, and she fed Oliver one spoonful at a time.

The power of the powerless. Which girl would you marry? Today Roe and I have three children.

Chapter III

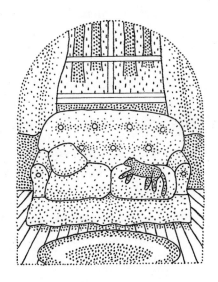

I had completed the article for the *Reader's Digest.*

"It's in the mail," I said to Roe as I lifted the covers of our bed, kissed her good night, and then I slept.

Roe was pregnant with our third child. David was five; Karen two. I had enough to anticipate with joy and worry, so I had little time to think about the magazine's reaction to the article.

The baby was kicking inside my wife; David was asking me to make a bow-and-arrow set. Karen was not yet sleeping through the night. I was grading one hundred papers every other week for my high school students.

Then, at the end of February, 1985, the *Digest* returned my story with suggestions for a revision. I was disappointed.

That night Roe and I spoke, rather Roe spoke to me about the article, about editors, patience, the ability to work with people, divergent opinions, acceptance. She spoke to me about these things. I wanted to tear up my article and forget the whole thing. Instead, I accepted Roe's advice, thought about it all for a few days, and then, finally, I sent the *Reader's Digest* a two-sentence reply:

Dear Sir:

Thank you for the time you spent reading the piece on Oliver, and for the time you spent writing your response.

I will see what I can do with the article.

And what I did that very same day was to send a two-sentence letter to *The Wall Street Journal:*

Dear Sir:

Enclosed is a piece I wrote this month. I think it might speak to many people, this message of hope, this message of triumph.

During the next month I waited for a reply from the *Journal,* and I made an attempt at rewriting the article for the *Reader's Digest.* Also, during that month, Roe gave birth to Michael, our ten-pound, seven-ounce boy, our second son.

"Wall Street Journal."

"Hello. This is Chris de Vinck. I sent an article to your office about a month ago, and I was wondering if any decision had been made?"

"Just a minute, please. I'll connect you with the editorial page."

"Thank you."

The phone clicked. I was on hold.

"Mr. de Vinck?"

"Yes."

"This is John Fund. We're interested in your article, but it is too long. I'll let you know by the end of the week if we can use it."

"Thanks very much."

At the end of the week, Barbara Phillips, an associate editor from the editorial desk, called.

"Mr. de Vinck. We would like to run your article about your brother sometime next week, but we have to cut it. We just don't have the space on the page to print the whole piece."

Do you remember Clarence, the guardian angel in the Frank Capra film *It's a Wonderful Life?* Clarence changed George's life.

Do you remember in Shakespeare's play how Friar John neglected to deliver Friar Laurence's letter to Romeo? Friar John's action turned the stars against Romeo.

We can all look back to a particular moment and say, yes, this event changed my life, or, yes this person helped me become who I am today.

When I met Roe . . . yes, that was one of those extraordinary moments. When our three children were born . . . those events changed my life. When I read the poetry of William Carlos Williams and the novel *To Kill a Mockingbird,* I grew.

And when Barbara Phillips selected my essay from the pile of unsolicited pieces that were spread upon her desk, when she thought something ought to be done with my story, my life changed, though I didn't know it at the time.

I was disappointed the story had to be cut down somewhat, but at least, I thought, that message of hope and joy would seep through just a bit anyway.

And so, on April 10, 1985, *The Wall Street Journal* ran on their Op/Ed page a small essay about my small, insignificant brother which they titled "Power of the Powerless: A Brother's Lesson." I was grateful.

I have learned over the years that a writer does not write in isolation. A career is not successful without the help of others. I was pleased to join Emily Dickinson and write in my basement room, mostly poetry, and keep all my finished work in the desk drawer. I kept my writing to myself like I kept the name of my first girlfriend hidden from my family, but then, after ten years of writing poetry, something happened, something I still cannot explain, except to say I discovered a hunger to share my writing with other people. I suddenly understood that I might be able to accomplish more with the typewriter than I might be able to accomplish in the classroom.

A true writer is a teacher, first, last and always a teacher. I have come to believe there is a joy, a something which I can bring up from my typewriter which might make a difference in the world. We *all* arrive at this moment. To believe it is in us, and to act upon that notion, defines who we are.

I will be forever grateful to Tim Ferguson, the editorial features editor of *The Wall Street Journal.* He was the first person to print any prose of mine. He had published the year before a piece I wrote about my growing up with people telling me stories, and how wonderful I thought that was. Tim was also the one who decided to print the story about Oliver.

The tough, precise *Wall Street Journal,* Barbara Phillips, Tim Ferguson, John Fund thought I could write. It took me three years from that moment to believe it.

The night Oliver's essay ran in the *Journal,* I received a phone call from one of the editors at the New York *Post.* I didn't catch his name.

"We would like to reprint your article in tomorrow's edition of the *Post.* Could we send a photographer to your house for a picture of you and your family?"

I wasn't sure what he was talking about.

"We would like a picture. We'd like to run the article about Oliver in the *Post.* "

I remember the man had a British accent, and he was very kind, in a hurry, but kind.

"Yes. O.K., I guess."

"Good. Let me connect you with our photographer. Thanks very much. By the way. Has the White House contacted you yet?"

"Ah, excuse me?" I asked.

"Oh. Well I guess I've told you more than you should know at the moment. We've just heard that the White House is trying to get in touch with you."

I felt at that moment the way Dorothy felt when she stepped out of her demolished house after it landed in Oz.

"No," I said. "No one has called."

"Let me connect you to our photography department. Thanks again," and he hung up.

I could not guess at the time what Oliver did to the nation on that day of April 10, 1985. I was soon to learn the task Oliver was still carrying out, though he had been dead for five years. I was soon to learn about the power of the powerless all over again.

It was a wonderful thing to know that my words sat on millions of people's laps as they returned home from a difficult day at work. Let no writer lose sight of his task. What was I getting myself into? I called *The Wall Street Journal*.

"Hello. This is Chris de Vinck."

"Hello, Chris," Barbara answered. "Congratulations."

For what, I thought. They printed my article.

"I just received a call from the *Post*, and they want to run my essay about Oliver tomorrow. Is that all right? I don't know much about the *Post*, or how things are done. And they want pictures."

Barbara reassured me that the *Post* often reprints things from the *Journal*.

"What they want to do, Chris, is a good thing. Their editorial page is highly respected."

"Well good," I answered weakly. "Oh, and Barbara, a fellow at the *Post* said something about the White House. I wonder if you know anything about that."

"Oh you found out. We were trying to keep it as a surprise. Yes, someone from the White House called to acquire your address and number. The President wants to call you, or write you a letter. He read your essay this morning."

"The President?"

Barbara spoke calmly. "I've been working on the *Journal*'s editorial page for two years, and I don't remember the White House having called us on anything we printed."

Well, Oliver, I thought. You have the power to move the President of the United States.

I hung up the phone and stepped into the living room where Roe was nursing Michael, our newborn son.

"Roe, ah, the New York *Post* would like to take a picture of us."

"I hope you said no."

For a moment I wished I had.

"Well, I said O.K."

"Chris. You know how nervous I am about that sort of thing. And we should have discussed it first. How could you."

"Yes, but it's a good thing. I called the *Journal.*"

"Well, all right. What day are they going to take the picture?"

"In an hour."

"An hour!"

"The photographer is already on his way from New York."

"Chris! Look at me!" Michael was still nursing. "Look at this house. Where is he going to take this picture? Look at this couch. An hour?"

I tried to reassure Roe that the holes in the couch weren't that noticeable and that she looked lovely.

Roe smiled, carried Michael to his crib, then she walked upstairs to dress.

"Ah, Roe," I called up. "I also think we're going to hear from the President."

"Fine," she called down. "Is he coming in an hour too?"

Ever do something without mentioning it to your husband or wife first?

"Really, Roe. The *Journal*, Barbara, said the President might call or write a letter."

We spent the next moments collecting the children's toys and pushing magazines and shoes under the couch.

"Should we have something for the photographer? Cake?"

"The oatmeal cookies you made yesterday are just fine."

The doorbell rang half an hour later.

"Hello. I'm from the New York *Post.*"

"Yes. Come in. Yes."

The camera, the bag full of equipment. The conversation.

"Where would you like to take the picture?" I asked.

"How about if you and your wife sit on the couch."

The couch.

"Maybe you could hold the baby? Do you have any more children?"

"Yes. We have a son and a daughter. They just went to bed." I walked up to their bedroom.

"Karen. Come downstairs just for a minute. A friend is going to take a picture of all of us."

"O.K., Daddy." Any excuse to get out of bed.

"David. There's a friend of mine downstairs who would like to take our picture. Would you like to come with Karen and me just for a minute?"

"Can I take Whiskers?"

Whiskers is the plush toy cat I had bought David two years earlier.

"Yes, of course you can bring Whiskers."

On April 11, 1985, on page seven of the New York *Post* above

Oliver's article, there was a half-page photograph of me, Roe, Karen, David, newborn Michael and Whiskers all sitting on the couch my wife and I had bought eight years before during the first days of our marriage. It was torn and faded, but functional.

Chapter IV

Five years before, in the spring of 1980, my two brothers and I had carried Oliver's coffin on one side, and three of the Weston monks were on the other side.

We walked from the small chapel, along a narrow road, up a hill, and through the cemetery. Behind us, the rest of the family followed as the monks sang their songs of triumph and joy.

I remember our placing the coffin on the ropes and wood slats above the open grave.

I remember our pulling out the wood and grasping the ropes. We slowly lowered Oliver's coffin to the bottom of the grave, pulled the ropes up, and began to pass the shovel around.

First my mother, then my father. We took turns collecting

earth and stones on the plate of the shovel, then turning it all into the dark hole.

I will never forget the sound the stones made as they hit and bounced on the metal coffin.

I will never forget the way my mother waved the shovel slowly back and forth as she scattered the moist earth across the opened ground. This is good, I thought.

"Chris," my wife greeted me as I came home from school on the afternoon of April 11, the day after my article was printed in the *Journal.* "CBS television wants you to call them back. They want to know if the President is going to call. Also, WABC radio called. A woman there would like you to join her on a Sunday night talk show."

What have I done, I thought. What has Oliver done?

In the early evening, I received a phone call from Dorothy Robinowitz, editor and columnist of the New York *Post.* I had never met Dorothy before, yet she took the time to call me from her desk at the *Post.*

"Christopher," she said. (Many people called me by my first name after they read Oliver's article.)

"Christopher, I'd like to congratulate you on your fine article about your brother Oliver."

One of the true pleasures of being a writer is receiving surprise phone calls, or receiving a letter from a reader.

"Christopher, I'd like to warn you about something. You're young. You are just starting to write. Stick to the literary. Don't get trapped into writing articles for the women's magazines. Your essay has the cadence and structure of literary quality. I was an English teacher too. Stick to the literary."

Of all the things that were said about my article, this was the one which brought me the greatest joy. Maybe, I thought, I am a writer. Maybe I can bring more to the surface.

When I was a boy I had a cat named Geisha. When I came home from school each day she would be waiting for me on the front porch. When I took a walk through the woods, she followed me. Each night before I went to bed, I stepped out upon the grass of the backyard and called loudly into the darkness, "Geisha! Geisha! Here Geisha, Geisha, Geisha!"

In the distance I heard the movement of dried leaves. I could tell she was running toward me: sometimes up from the swamp, sometimes from the back of the chicken coop; always toward me and into my arms, then I carried her up to bed.

One night I called and called, waiting to hear the familiar sounds of my cat running in the night.

"Geisha!" I called. I listened.

"Geisha!" I stopped as I heard the quick, faint repeating of her name. It was my echo, weak, but my echo just the same bouncing off the neighbor's barn three houses away. It was not the first time I'd noticed it, but it was the first time I realized that if my voice had the strength to move across the yard, into the fields, and return to me, then other people in the neighborhood could surely hear my cry, and I was embarrassed. From that night on, I clapped my hands together. I never sang out for my cat again.

Why do we reach an age where we are embarrassed to be heard? The tragedy is that too many of us carry that embarrassment into our adulthoods.

Years later, as a graduate student at Columbia University, I began to write my first poems. They were, at first, my private attempts at replacing a girl I had loved and lost, but then something else took hold. I suddenly wasn't ashamed to call out into the darkness any longer.

I wrote and I wrote from January 1974 through the spring, two, three, sometimes four poems a day, and what was strange, I remembered all the poems without making any attempts at memorizing them. They just stayed with me, nearly sixty in all by the time I graduated.

That summer I spent two weeks with my parents in Canada along the shore of the Madawaska River in central Ontario.

The first day we rented a small motorboat. That afternoon I took the boat out upon the old river. I was alone. It occurred to me that this would be a fine place to hear how my poems sounded aloud. I was certain the noise of the engine and the distance from the shore guaranteed my privacy.

I spoke out in dramatic rhymes and inflections as the boat and I advanced down the middle of the river passing distant bathers, a fisherman on a dock, girls on the beach sunning themselves.

I nearly sang my poems above the sound of the engine's roar, then I turned the rudder and sped back home.

Full of sun and peace, I sat upon the beach with a book: *The Collected Poems of W. B. Yeats.* Moments later I heard another boat, much like my own, passing before me at some distance. Above the rattle and sputter of their engine, I heard three teen-agers laughing and talking. I clearly heard every word they said: "Do you want to keep going? I got money. Let's buy some soda in town."

I didn't know sound carried so well over water. No wonder people on the distant shore looked up or waved to me as I passed earlier before them during my "private" poetic incantations. I felt foolish.

After that summer I began my career as a teacher. It took me three years to realize that the closer I came to exposing my heart, the louder I called out what I saw and what I felt, the more my students listened.

Now, as a writer, I try each night at my desk to push out into the darkness and across the water the sound of my voice, hoping someone will wave back, or shout, like my echo, a greeting: "Yes! Hello! I have felt that way too!"

I believe it is this we seek in America today, that desire to cry out as Walt Whitman did in his poem "To a Stranger":

"Passing stranger! You do not know how longingly I look upon you."

I tried to explain these things as best I could to my new friend at the New York *Post*. "I've been writing poetry for ten years," I told Dorothy. "If I were to choose a type of writing I'd like to do for a living, it would be the writing of poetry, but I also like the essays."

I explain to Dorothy a bit about my poetry. We spoke about literature, about writing columns, about teaching.

"If you ever need help, call. Send me some things you write in the future," she offered. "Let's meet for lunch someday. Don't call me on Thursdays. That's when I am working on my column."

Because of Oliver, I met this kind woman. For a writer to receive unbidden words of encouragement, for anyone to receive unbidden words of encouragement, this is the material a true gift is made of.

Today, in Oliver's room, my mother has a small metal crucifix on the pillow of his well-made empty bed. The wall is still slightly stained from small bits of food Oliver used to spit out which he didn't like: strained peas or mashed potatoes.

Still in Oliver's room, there is an image which appears and disappears as I slowly open and close my eyes.

I remember exactly where every tree stood in our yard. I remember where the original kitchen table stood which my father built to accommodate our large family. Everything had its place when we were children: fixed, certain, familiar.

The southeastern corner of Oliver's room was his place, his continent. When he died, when his coffin was passed through the open window of the living room, the window that had never been open in my lifetime, Oliver's room became a photograph fixed in the frame of his empty bed, and shut dresser, and fading curtains—a snapshot I carry with me.

I constantly walk between the memory of my brother, my family, my childhood on one side, and the future and my own death on the other.

Outside Oliver's bedroom there was a long hallway which separated our bedrooms: one on the left and three on the right. It was a narrow, insignificant hall until one summer afternoon, while my parents were shopping and my brothers and sisters were about the house reading, or painting, or playing "Go Fish," I discovered, all at once, that I could press my left hand and leg against one wall, and press my right hand and leg against the opposite wall and work my way to the ceiling like a spider climbing between two parallel struts of its web.

For days, each time I made my climb, I was afraid someone might hear the loud thud as I let go and dropped back down to the hard floor.

Eventually I let my sister Anne in on my secret, and she joined me on occasions for our personal, Mary Poppins-like conversations as we were pressed between the two walls with our heads two or three inches from the ceiling. I remember how we laughed and laughed and laughed.

That experience is one of the first times I can remember being wedged between something in a significant way, though as a child the only significance I could understand was the strong reprimand I'd receive from my parents if my shoeprints were ever discovered up and along the high walls. They never were.

How often do we experience an insignificant moment which, later in our lives, returns to us in a significant different color?

Today, without expecting to be, I find myself again wedged between two different walls holding me up: my own children and my parents. I sense, suddenly, the balance of the generations pulling me from both sides. This middle position carries its own significance. What I do not know rests in the wisdom of my father and mother, and what I do know is revealed to me in the small actions of my three children.

I sometimes wish I could be my father, but I know the dangers a reflected image holds; sometimes I wish I could be my son, but I know the dangers of smothering new hope.

We all dare to step out beyond our middle existence: above what we can do, and below to where we have already been.

I remember the Saturday I drove to Howe Caverns in New York State with a few high school friends when I was a teenager. We longed for things to do, and a trip down an elevator through solid rock to look at stalactites and stalagmites seemed sensible enough.

As we stepped out from the elevator and into the cavern, I remember thinking about being below the surface, away from the light and parents and teachers, and I learned that this stepping below all that I had come to know offered nothing more than darkness, moisture and little sound except for the echo of my own voice.

I was pleased to return to the surface that afternoon after walking through layers of earth below the ordinary day.

The darkness in the cavern revealed its own truth to me as did my journey up in the opposite direction toward the sun many years later when I felt myself rise above the middle ground.

Last fall my mother coordinated her first garage sale. Thirty years of tools, chairs, dressers, clocks, clothes and toys were pulled out of the house to the front lawn. Roe and I spent the day with my parents pricing each item with white labels, carrying objects for customers, collecting money.

After the morning rush of bargain hunters had subsided, there was a pause in business, so Roe and my mother returned to the house for lunch and warmth. My father raked a few leaves; the children climbed in and out of the rhododendron bushes, and I decided to climb the front pine tree which I hadn't done in twenty years.

The climb was difficult. Dead branches and new branches blocked my smooth ascent. After a few moments of twisting and pulling I managed to reach the top of the tree which swayed back and forth with my weight.

From the top of the tree I realized it had grown taller than the three-story house, the house where I learned how to say my own name. The last time I climbed the tree, the top reached the second floor. Twenty years later the house, my home, was suddenly smaller, and I was taller, above the roof of my childhood. I swayed, nearly like a madman, high above my father and my mother and my wife and my children, and I didn't like it.

We can easily step beyond our families, look up to a high adventure, sway among the treetops and fly away into the burning sun, but I climbed back down.

The pine sap stuck to my hands for a few days, reminding me of my guilt, my trespassing beyond and above what I have come to believe is the center, the middle of our true existence: homes, mothers, fathers, wives and children.

During the last few years as a writer I have slowly discovered where the best material can be found: in the middle. There is the great joy of love on the one side, and the great sadness of hate on the other. Both extremes exist in our common, everyday world, but we cannot walk through deep caverns in darkness all our lives, nor can we rise above the neighborhood and disappear into the blinding light. It is this flat ground where we name our children after ourselves and make excuses to our parents. It is the combination of darkness and light, the shadows, this middle earth where we harbor our true passions.

The best we can do is wedge ourselves between the walls.

Chapter V

Oliver could not say his name or any word in any language. He could not gesture approval or dismay. He could not lift his own hands. He could not see. Helpless? Useless? Burden? Shame?

Give me your weak and your suffering. We the people. To form a more perfect nation. We hold these truths. In God we trust. Oliver. Simple. My brother. All men are created equal. The power of the powerless.

Dear Mr. de Vinck:

It is not often, in reading the daily newspapers, that I come across an article as moving as the one you wrote for the April 10 *Wall Street Journal.*

We sometimes fall into the habit of thinking that the weakest among us, like your brother Oliver, are a burden we must stoically bear. But you show that they can teach us the deepest lessons of love. Your essay will help many people to recognize this truth.

Nancy joins me in sending our best wishes for the future. God bless you.

Sincerely,
Ronald Reagan

And the letters came and came.

Dear Mr. de Vinck:

Obviously I don't have your address, otherwise I wouldn't be writing to you in care of *The Wall Street Journal.* I am hoping, however, that this letter will reach you because I have just read your stirring essay "Power of the Powerless."

My wife started Special Olympics 18 years ago. Since that time she and I have read scores of articles about the mentally retarded, but I can't remember any single story more moving than yours. So, I just wanted to write a letter of congratulations to you, and a letter of thanks for all the love you gave to Oliver, but most of all for sharing your experience with the public at large.

Would you give Special Olympics permission to make copies of your article and mail them to all the people who are helping us so much with our Olympians? I hope you will let us share with them the inspiration Oliver gave to you.

Kindest regards,
Sargent Shriver

Dear Mr. de Vinck:

Fr. John Ahearn shared with me your article which was printed in *The Wall Street Journal* earlier this year and then reprinted in the New York *Post.* Your words are a beautiful testimony to the value of human life and to the need for love in the home. I thank you for providing this kind of inspiration to those who have had the opportunity to read your beautiful message.

May God continue to bless you, Roe, and your children.

> Bishop Rodimer
> Paterson, New Jersey

To the Editor:

The message from Mr. de Vinck amongst the acquisitions, divestitures and "wheeling-dealings" reported in the *Journal* is clear. We should all take an inventory of ourselves and of our dealings with other people and try and remember what is really important about life.

The character and compassion of the human soul is still number one.

> Sincerely,
> Melvin Schlechter
> New York

Dear Mr. de Vinck:

The Wall Street Journal carried a short article by you on Wednesday, April 10th, which touched me deeply.

Not only was I affected by the human quality of your story, but obviously I have a professional interest, as my work involves fund raising and administration for a center of multihandicapped blind children in Israel.

I would like to ask for your permission to send this article to some of our friends in the American community as a heartwarming demonstration of human compassion.

Yours,
Paul H. Goldenberg
Kern Or, New York, N.Y.

Dear Mr. de Vinck:

I would not hold it against your first girl who declined to visit your brother. Some people are just constituted that way. They can't take it. I am one of them.

Cordially,
Jack Kahn
Florida

Dear Mr. de Vinck:

It's very seldom that I'm moved to tears, but your article moistened the eyes of even a macho guy like me. It was so inspiring to read about all the love, courage, perseverance, and insight demonstrated by your parents in caring at home for thirty-three years your bedridden, blind and retarded Oliver. Two parts of the article were especially touching and significant.

After learning that Oliver could not be cured and being told by the doctor that Oliver could be put in an institution, your parents replied, "But he is our son. We will take Oliver home, of course." Maybe it's because I'm the father of a two-year-old boy and am particularly sensitive about things like this, but I also think that the impact of "of course" is due to the fact that it is a succinct repudiation of the looming "quality of life" argument and all its slippery slope manifestations. The "of course" is a pithy and confident affirmation of the worthiness of all human life.

Additionally, you remember how your mother explained that Oliver was a blessing in ways that were not immediately apparent? What a refreshing contrast to the compassionate crowd which views handicapped people (born and unborn) as inconvenient, cursed, burdensome, and less valuable.

R. Michael Key
Illinois

To the Editor:

What is seldom discussed is the fact that "Oliver" and those like him have a "right to life" and dignity irrespective of the values of an individual family. Baby Doe was probably more than a "vegetable," but because family and doctors had no such reverence for the sanctity of life— only life whose criteria met theirs—Baby Doe starved to death in the corner of a hospital.

How true it is that those who ignore history are condemned to relive it! In 1920, the book *The Release of the Distruction of Life Devoid of Value* was published in Germany. It was not the beginning of the quality of life "ethic" but the crystallization of it. As a result of this book —or the ethic distilled in this book, the elite (doctors, psychiatrists, professors, lawyers) began destroying "life devoid of value." This included retarded, handicapped, aged, permanently injured World War I veterans—all useless eaters! Hitler has taken a bum rap! His holocaust was only an extension of their portable gassing machines— expanding them into the extermination camps which not only killed six million Jews, but another six million including Gypsies, Slavs, and other "inferior" types of people. Why, I ask, is the holocaust of the 30's and 40's referred to specifically as the "Jewish" holocaust? Why must the stigma of the holocaust be thrust uniquely upon the Germans? The late Frederic Wertham stated in his book *A Sign for Cain, an Explanation of Human Violence* that this holocaust was "not strictly a national matter, for the perpetrators had no difficulty in finding collaborators— even active ones—in other countries. It is not a past historical episode, because it is still largely unresolved legally, politically, psychologically, and educationally. It was not a disorderly orgy of primitive violence, but a mass action lasting years and carried out with pedantic orderliness."

Is this "quality of life" ethic not still alive and growing in influence everyday in the elite universities and societies? Is this "quality of life" in fact not the prevailing ethic of Western Civilization at the present time? Are there not many so-called Jewish and Christian churches who adamantly support it? What is meant by "population control"? Things have, in fact, deteriorated to the point where parents are delivering their children up freely and requesting their elimination. Who said that Hitler didn't win the war?

Sincerely,
Demain Whiteside
California

To the Editor:

Compassion, commitment, and above all—love and understanding given from one human being to another— transcends all of her human endeavors.

Very truly yours,
Russell Adkins
Texas

Dear Christopher and Roe:

My name is Gertrude. I'm 64 years old. I have two wonderful children: James and Kathleen, 7 grandchildren and one more due in a week.

I have a husband who is 74 and has Alzheimer's Disease and he is now my baby.

> Gertrude Feeney
> New York

Dear Sirs:

Thank you for giving prime editorial space to Oliver, and giving us the opportunity to stop and reflect on the true "quality of life"—compassion, love, kindness and that depth of human sadness and suffering that really serves as the backdrop for genuine joy.

> Sincerely,
> Stuart W. Ferguson
> Williamsburg, Virginia

To the Editor:

Several years ago while visiting in Des Moines, my wife and I listened to the celebrant of mass at a small parish church as he delivered a homily on the canonization of Elizabeth Seton, reminding us to listen to the rites which were to be televised that day via satellite from Rome.

In his remarks, the priest told us how thrilling it was to him personally, for he had walked the very same cobblestone streets as a seminarian and this in the very century that she had. Her canonization then was not like reading about some ancient ascetic poring over dusty tomes in a walled-in monastery eons ago. On the contrary, Elizabeth Seton was a symbol to him, and should be to us all. Of the many saints around us, doing without a cry or whimper the ordinary and indeed, the extraordinary tasks of the day, unsung and unheralded, with "no time to be vigilling or watching the twilight dawn or storming heaven's gate," but rather to be a "saint by getting meals and washing up the plates," and I add, changing and powdering and feeding the baby as well as the old and feeble.

The homilist did not doubt that in that congregation and in other congregations across the land, that there were many Latter-day Saints and we had only to look around us.

Thank you for printing the homily in *The Wall Street Journal* about heroes, aye, about saints, whose good deeds, like the little candle's beam, shine in a naughty world.

> Sincerely,
> George Sullivan
> Illinois

Oliver could not move his own hands, could not wink, whisper, stand. He did not have the power to hold a spoon, to write a letter, to embrace; yet he had the power to move the President of the United States, a former vice-presidential candidate, bishops, Jewish leaders, doctors, mechanics, lawyers, carpet salesmen, corporate secretaries.

During the following months, Oliver's article was reprinted in the following publications: *Reader's Digest, Catholic Digest,* the Chicago *Sun,* the New York *Post, Read Magazine, New Covenant, Catholic New York, Campus Life.* I was invited to speak on radio stations and to appear on television, and letter after letter found their way to my cluttered desk.

What moves a man or woman to lift a pen and write a letter? Poets know the music of that secret. Novelists understand the story. We *all* possess universal insights which, on the surface, appear to be just ordinary moments. Those involved in the arts attempt to make ordinary things extraordinary, and they try to make extraordinary things ordinary.

"Every moment is a window on all time," Thomas Wolfe wrote in his novel *Look Homeward, Angel.* When that moment is brought to our attention, we stop what we are doing and sing or dance or dream or write a poem or compose a symphony or write a letter.

I have come to realize that what is most personal, central to our private lives, is so universal in us all.

During my first years as a teacher, I was very closemouthed to my high school students about my love for my wife, about the delight I take in the sound of a robin during the early dusk. I hesitated before I told my students about how lonely I used to be in college, or how I say aloud in my car while driving to work, "Thank you God for Roe and the children."

One reason I didn't share these things was because I did not want to be laughed at. As the years passed, I realized that these are the things young people *long* to hear. I realized that the most important things in me were the most important things to teach. I believe a teacher should be a spiritual, political, social and intellectual role model who speaks about love and justice and Hamlet.

One sadness I see in these modern times is our attempt to try and keep ourselves private, hidden, aloof. I believe we must return to the secret of ourselves and slowly unlock the closed doors. Who we are will be revealed again and again in the most unlikely places like, perhaps, in the Op/Ed pages of *The Wall Street Journal.*

"I liked that beetle, Daddy."

"You mean he was a vegetable?"

"God has chosen the weak things of the world to confound the things which are mighty."

"But he is our son. We will take him home, of course."

"Which girl would you marry?"

I often think of Charles Dickens' *Christmas Carol,* and Marley's ghost returning to Scrooge to warn him. I think about the three spirits showing Ebenezer the things he left behind in the world of the past and present.

Oliver taught me to live in the past, present and in the future. His condition was a constant reminder to me of what he might have been, what he was, and what he would become: a saint.

That is part of the mystery. Like the transformed Scrooge at the end of the story, Oliver's own heart laughed, and that was quite enough for him, but my vision had to be focused to see this laughter. I learned that the spirit of Oliver, past, present and future lives within me, within us all. Oliver was physically and mentally retarded, but he was not spiritually retarded.

I was taught by my parents to look at Oliver and *see.* I was able to take what I saw, arrange the colors, days, years, and write an essay. The spirit of Oliver, the icon of Oliver left an image on the page of *The Wall Street Journal,* an icon we all clearly see: the mystery, things that linger, things which stay with us. The Holy Spirit. We can stand before the Olivers of the world and see clearly who we are.

Chapter VI

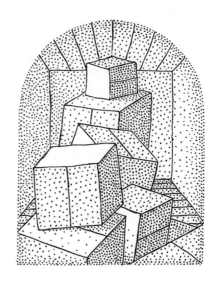

Dear Mr. de Vinck:

Thank you for your moving story "Power of the Powerless: A Brother's Lesson." It was a year ago that our second child, a daughter, was born. My wife and I are sure we would have shared many happy moments with her too. The morning she was born we had expected a normal delivery and a healthy, happy baby. The reality was very different. When Lauren (our baby's name) gasped her first breath, she inhaled a large amount of meconium.

While my wife recovered from the delivery that morning, I spent the remainder of that day and night watching and waiting in the special care nursery. I wondered how this could happen to people like us. My wife and I are not perfect, but we had always thought of ourselves as good people. Had we done something to deserve this? And what about Lauren? What had she done? I suppose we all ask these questions when the worst happens.

As Lauren lay on the little bed with doctors hurrying all around, a kindly nurse said, "Mr. Guilbault, you can touch your baby." I reached out clumsily and Lauren squeezed my little finger and I looked into her eyes. I wanted to tell her that if she got better I would be the best daddy she could find.

The next afternoon Lauren died, and the doctor let me hold her in my arms. Like your brother Oliver, Lauren was the most powerless person I have ever known. Without a respirator she would not have lived at all. Yet in her short life she had the power to change mine forever.

When I think of Lauren, I do not think of how she suffered, but of how she grabbed my finger tightly and looked right into my eyes as I stared into hers. In her eyes I saw beauty and love. I often wonder what she saw in mine.

Peter R. Guilbault
Rhode Island

This is the mystery, things that linger. We can look into the eyes of Lauren, we can look into the eyes of Oliver and see who we are.

What did Lauren see in the eyes of her father? What did Oliver "see" through the caress and voice of my mother? There is something hidden inside the chairs, the walls, in the clocks.

"There are more things in heaven and earth, Horatio, than are dreamt of in your philosophy." William Shakespeare knew of this seeing. Everything has an inside, and that inside is never exactly defined despite science and philosophy.

When I received all these letters, when I received this letter from Lauren's father, I realized I had stumbled into the mystery, fallen inside the lingering dust which is the stuff of great literature, and art, and music: life and love, of course.

What would you have done with Mr. Guilbault's letter? With all the letters? Well, I answered them, nearly one hundred in all, but there was something in a number of these letters, something I could not just fold and place inside my metal filing cabinet.

Many people sent me letters about the powerless people in their lives. A woman wrote about her husband with Alzheimer's Disease. A corporate secretary wrote about tending to her sick grandmother for fourteen years. A couple from Washington, D.C., wrote about their child who was born with half his brain out of his skull. A mother wrote from Florida about her son who was just like Oliver. A minister from Seattle wrote about his brother with Down's Syndrome. Peter Guilbault wrote a letter to me about his daughter, Lauren.

What could I do with these letters, I thought. Better still: What do I *have* to do with these letters? I followed the paths which were opening to me.

I recognized in these letters the community of suffering, and the community of love, these things which touch us all. I decided to bring together the people I had met because of Oliver. Oliver brought Peter Guilbault to me. I'll go to Peter. Oliver brought Lauren into my life. Well, I will go see what I can make of this little girl who lived for just a single day.

I wrote a letter to Mr. Guilbault explaining my idea for this book, and he invited me to his home.

As I drove to Rhode Island, I wondered just how far I dare aim toward the inside. How far would I be allowed to go with an interview with these people, Peter and Barbara, this young couple who wrote me after reading about Oliver in the newspaper?

How often do we go to social gatherings with friends and never scratch the surface of who anyone really is?

Here I was, asking two strangers if I could come into their home, if I could sit at their table and listen to them talk about one of the most important, tender, painful things in their lives.

Where there is pain and memory, there are those things which linger: a sore, a hurt, colors, sounds . . . but, too, an alchemy . . . that alchemy in sorrow. "It can be transmuted," says Pearl Buck. "It can be transmuted into wisdom, which if it does not bring joy, can yet bring happiness."

I wanted to see if this couple would give you and me the wisdom, the gift of themselves. Would they share with us those things which lingered long after their day old baby died?

Here, in the words of her father, is *all* that is left of Lauren Guilbault. Here is the power she holds.

*   *   *

Just after Lauren died, our doctor sent one of his nurses home who lived near the hospital to get a camera. He took a picture of Lauren as she was stretched out on this small platform. It wasn't a bed really, just some soft padding and sheets. She was strapped down with all the tubes and lights.

The doctor apologized about the quality of the picture. It was awfully nice of him because we don't have anything else of her.

Part of the way I dealt with Lauren's death was to fish around in medical books. I had never heard of meconium. A baby's first stools are formed while she is still inside the mother. After the baby is born, she soon passes her first bowel movement which is black and tarlike. Meconium.

When Barbara went into labor after nine normal months of her pregnancy, for one reason or another Lauren went into stress before she was born. She wasn't getting enough oxygen. Maybe the cord was around her neck and, just like a reflex, Lauren passed her first bowel movement while she was still inside Barbara.

A baby constantly inhales fluids in the amniotic sac, but the blood vessels in the baby's lungs are constricted so none of the material hurts the baby.

When Lauren was born, just when she took her first breath, she inhaled, gasped, and the meconium was sucked into her mouth and lungs. It was like inhaling molasses. The little air sacs and capillaries in the lungs never opened.

I was in the waiting room because Barbara was scheduled to have a cesarean. I'm squeamish, so Barbara and I decided the best place for me would be in the waiting room.

I saw this nurse come flying out of the delivery room followed by a doctor and the pediatrician. I followed as they brought Lauren to that glass place where they care for newborns . . . the nursery. Lauren looked normal to me. There seemed to be absolutely nothing wrong with her. She was moving around.

The doctor stepped out of the nursery. "There's a slight problem with the baby. She inhaled meconium. It is quite common, and generally there is not much of a problem, but as a precaution I'd like to send Lauren to Providence to the Women and Infant Hospital Special Care Nursery."

That is when I got a little upset. I wanted to cry.

"No, no, Mr. Guilbault. It will be just for a couple of days. The baby can come back here soon with your wife."

"All right."

Within half an hour the team from Women and Infant's came to pick up Lauren. They took some X rays. I held my daughter.

I watched the doctor as he examined Lauren's X rays.

"Mr. Guilbault. Your baby is going to be very, very sick."

I gave up Lauren from my cradled arms to the medical team. By the time I reached the Women and Infant Hospital, after I saw Barbara, they already had Lauren strapped on that little plat-

form which looks like a small bed. She didn't have any diaper.
She was conscious.

I looked around the Special Care Nursery and saw all these
other babies. Most of them were premature. Some had cleft
palates. As I looked at the babies I was amazed that they were
alive. Some of the premature babies were so small.

Lauren was eight pounds. A pretty good-sized baby, healthy
and kicking and everything else. Her color was off a little. She
was blue.

When they brought her in to see me, she had that washed out
blue look. The doctor asked me to leave for a minute because he
wanted to connect Lauren to a respirator.

I stepped out into the hall and had a cigarette, then I was
allowed back in. Things got pretty bad. I was told by the doctors
that they were taking X rays of Lauren every hour, and she was
getting worse.

Lauren was attached to the respirator with that thing that goes
up and down, and this beep-beep-beep machine like you see on
television. She was wired up.

The doctor kept telling me that she was going to get a lot sicker
before she was going to get any better. I was amazed by the
honesty of these good people. They never made me think that,
yes, Lauren was going to be all right. They never said that. When
I tried to put those words into their mouths, they said, "No, Mr.
Guilbault. You had better listen. Your baby is by far the sickest
one in here."

I first found out that Barbara was pregnant on July 24, 1983.
That was a Thursday night. I was out with a friend.

We had been trying for a few months. Barbara went for a blood
test. She didn't tell me because she didn't want to bring my hopes
up. Barbara called the doctor that night and received the positive
results. She met me at the door. I remember her words. "I had a

blood test this afternoon, and the results are positive. I'm pregnant!"

I was stunned. Barbara thought I was disappointed. It just didn't set in at first. She had to repeat what she said. "I'm pregnant." I embraced her, then we started calling all the relatives.

I was happy, but it frightened me too. That's a big thing . . . so special and all. This was our first baby. I had been married before, and so had Barbara. She had one boy, Tommy. Lauren was our first, but I love Tommy. He's really my first, and will always be. Lauren was a different type of first for Barbara and me. It was scary.

A few days later I started thinking, "Can we afford it? Is the house big enough?" I was worrying about silly stuff like that.

There was a time when I first graduated from high school, when I went to Colby, that I never wanted to return to this little town. I wanted to live in the city and make lots of money.

When I graduated from college my whole thing was to make money. I had to get a job and make lots of money. I went out and drove a Mercedes. I had two. I went skiing at Vail. I thought, "I'm going to show everybody that I'm something." My whole value as a person was tied up in what I could buy.

The first time Barbara felt the baby moving we were watching television. It was at night and she didn't say anything because she thought it was just gas, that bubbly feeling. She thought I wouldn't be able to feel it on the outside. It was something only she could feel on the inside. She wanted to wait for the really big kicks, which there were plenty of later.

About four and a half months later, Barbara felt a flutter which she could recognize as a flutter. She was anxious. She wanted to wear maternity clothes right away.

We have a cousin like that. Brenda. If she is just planning to get pregnant, she starts wearing maternity clothes.

Barbara was more anxious about being pregnant this time. Her ex-husband and she were separated when Barbara was six months pregnant with Tommy, so she had had no one to share the pregnancy with, so this was almost a new thing. She had a husband and she was going to make him wait on her hand and foot, which I did gladly.

Barbara ate so much ice, I couldn't believe it. She is a big Coca-Cola freak. She loves ice in her soda. She'll fill the glass right up with ice. When I'd go to the freezer for ice, there wouldn't be any. Then I'd see glasses all around the house with small amounts of water left at the bottom.

Toward the end of her pregnancy, she had so much heartburn that ice seemed to be the only thing that would help. Her doctor wouldn't give her anything. He said not to take any laxatives or anything like that, so she chewed on ice, really chewed it. I kept telling her that she was going to ruin her teeth.

I remember when the baby started kicking. Barbara and I always took turns sleeping up against each other's backs. One night I got this slight pressing against my side. At first I thought it was Barbara.

"Did you feel that?" she said.

The baby.

She thought I wasn't too thrilled about the baby moving because I just sat there. Most people say, "Wow, you can feel the baby kick!" but I sat there thinking about what it means, that this baby was actually in Barbara. Where did it come from? What a strange miracle, or something. It was like a mystery to me. It wasn't like, "Oh, Barbara's going to have a baby. Great!" It wasn't a thing like that. It was a real mystery. A miracle-type thing.

I would try to picture what position the baby was in because I'd feel this lump come right up here and it would move away, and there'd be a lump on this side of Barbara. I didn't know if that was the baby's head or her elbow or what.

About a week before Lauren was born, there was a program on PBS from WNET, New York. The program was about birth. They showed the miracle of birth from before conception. They showed the baby inside the womb actually breathing in fluids.

We couldn't decide on a girl's name. For a boy it was going to be Steven Francis. I think we pretty much decided on that, but for a girl, we had no name picked out. We had a million picked out.

I wanted to call the girl Stevie. Barbara said, "I know why you like that name, because of the girl in the rock-'n'-roll group," but that wasn't the reason. I just liked that name. Then we thought about Stephanie and nicknaming her Stevie, but Barbara didn't like the name Stephanie.

Barbara is the one who named the baby. We went through a number of books, but then, did you ever see that television commercial with Lauren Bacall? Well, Barbara said, "Oh, Lauren. How pretty." It's not Laurie or Laura. Those were plain, but Lauren, that was just a little bit different.

After Lauren died, we had a difficult time telling Tommy.

"Mommy's gonna have other babies, Tommy. You might have another sister."

"I know," he said. "Mommy's gonna get fat. She's gonna get pregnant. She's gonna get fat, go to the hospital, and the baby's gonna die."

We told Tommy in the hospital that night. They took me down to a waiting room where Tommy was sitting all alone. Nobody else was in there. The room was poorly lit.

"Your sister isn't going to be coming home, Tommy."

"Why?"

The thing is, Barbara's parents are really religious. I think they wanted us to tell him something like, "God took your little sister away because he needed her up in heaven," or something like that. I didn't want to tell him that. It made God look so bad. I didn't want him being mad at God, or thinking that if he needed his sister more, maybe God would have left her with us, and then Tommy might feel guilty, like it was his fault that his sister died.

We just told Tommy, "Your sister won't be coming home. She died, Tommy."

"Why'd she die?"

"She was so sick nobody could help her."

"Well, I guess God didn't listen when I prayed."

I didn't know exactly what to say next. "She was so sick, Tommy, even God couldn't help her." That's what I told him because that's what I thought too. I didn't lie to him. That's what I thought.

I read a book once about a man whose life falls apart and somebody explains to him how life is like a beautiful tapestry, but only God can see the tapestry. Man looks at it from underneath and can't see the whole thing, but if man could be in God's position, he would be able to see the whole tapestry; he'd be able to see how everything fits together in a beautiful plan.

That sticks up for God an awful lot, but that doesn't help people who are left behind. And besides, what type of plan could God have with Lauren's death? How could that fit into a plan? What plan could be worth sacrificing a little baby?

I have seen people who were dead, but I never realized how fragile life is. What is it, the birth of life? It's so . . . when Lauren . . . later on that night I was praying, and I don't do that often, but I was praying, "Please God, make her better," like you would ask for something on a Christmas list. I guess everybody prays that way. They make a Christmas list, and when God doesn't give them what they want . . . that night with the medication and everything . . . they were doing what they called a blood-gas test every fifteen minutes on Lauren. It was about one o'clock in the morning. The doctor was showing me the results of all these tests.

"If she goes another twenty minutes like this," the doctor said, "you're going to have to make a decision. I'll help you make it."

He was telling me that he couldn't be sure, but if my daughter kept going the way she was going, there would surely be brain damage. There was a good possibility of it. Then my prayers were much different. They changed from, "Please make her better," to, "Help us, God, one way or another." I didn't know what to pray for.

When Lauren was dying, when she died, the next day I was mad, I guess. I thought, like Tommy said, "He didn't hear my prayers," but then I went to see Barbara. There were so many people who really cared what happened to us: the doctors, the nurses, our families, the people at work. The doctor who took the picture of Lauren just after she died, he didn't have to do that.

I guess, maybe, in another way God did hear my prayers because even though Lauren was gone, there were many people behind us who cared.

There were, of course, many people, even today who say, "I don't know why you want to talk about it. Just forget it. She died and she's gone. Just suppress it, or repress it." But I don't want to still be mad ten years from now. I don't want to be unable to talk about it, or have it all come out of me in another way, like suddenly I don't like children anymore because I lost one, and I could never face it.

My mother lost thirteen children. She had thirteen miscarriages. She wanted a little girl so badly, but she never had one.

Her last pregnancy was stillborn, but it *was* a girl.

People say to me, "Oh yes, I lost a girl five years ago, but we had others . . ." We lost one five years ago they say, as if it wasn't even a human being. That's why, just after Lauren died, I asked the doctor if I could hold her. I was hesitant about it because I was afraid he would think, "Well, why does he want to hold a dead baby?" But the doctor said, "By all means. We almost insist on it," which surprised me. "I want you to see, Peter, that she was a real human being. Your daughter."

At the funeral I took some pictures. Lauren is buried right on top of my father. The church won't let us write anything on the tombstone. We've been trying to do that, but the priest and the bishop won't let us write anything there. I wish we could. It's a family plot. My grandmother's name is already on the stone. You know how old people put their names on the stone even before they die?

She said if we wanted to have Lauren's name put on her stone, to have it written right under her name, but the priest said no. We just want Lauren's name.

I grew up thinking that, feeling funny about myself as if my father was this big strong man, and I was always a little runt. Growing up I wanted to be just like my father. I guess I just didn't think much of myself. I wanted to be popular and all that. I didn't think I was as good as other people, as smart as they were. I don't know. I like it in this town now. I like people.

Things hadn't been smooth for Barbara and me in the beginning. I used to have a drinking problem. I've been to those seminars for alcoholics for three years.

When I first met Barbara she thought I was so special. I told her all the stories about going to Colby, being in the Marine Corps. She couldn't believe I was twenty-eight years old and already had done so much. She was twenty.

I was never a daily drinker or anything like that, but what I said earlier about myself feeling something like I was less than my father. That probably hit my big ego. When things didn't go my way, when life threw me a curveball, I drank. I wouldn't have to face anything. I was afraid Barbara might hurt me when I first met her, so I'd always hold something back.

When I read Oliver's story in *The Wall Street Journal,* the thing that struck me the most was the word "powerless" because at those seminars "powerlessness" is a very big item. That's the only way to stay sober for an alcoholic. You have to surrender to that. You have to acknowledge there is a higher power. That is what a sober alcoholic has to believe in, that there is a power greater than himself, be that my group meetings, or another person, or God. You have to accept that.

I was going ice fishing. I was supposed to be back to take Tommy to a Christmas party that afternoon for a Knights of Columbus holiday affair. I was going to be back by one o'clock so I could take Tommy. All the fathers were to bring their children.

I went ice fishing. I made a few holes in the ice just to say I went fishing. I didn't catch anything, then I went to a bar. I told myself that I had to be home by one o'clock. I had every intention of leaving so I could take Tommy to that Christmas party.

Of course, after three or four drinks, I didn't leave. I didn't care. That's the way it is with alcoholics. Once they take one drink, that's it.

I forgot all about Tommy and Barbara and all the things that mattered. I just thought about myself. I guess I got home the next morning. I already had it worked out in my mind how Barbara and I would have a fight for me being out all night and missing the party, and then I would go out to another bar. It was all worked out in my mind.

When I arrived home, I walked upstairs to change. My clothes smelled of beer and wine.

After I slipped my shoes on and my pants and shirt, I walked out into the hall only to see Tommy coming out of his bedroom. It was the morning. He just stared at me. He just stood in front of me and said, "Daddy?"

He was going to ask me a question. I looked down at him. Tommy was about two years old. He was really small. I guess I woke him up as I opened and closed my dresser drawers.

I just looked at him. He looked into my eyes, and that is when I saw myself for the first time. I looked in the mirror as I shaved every day for years, and I never saw what I saw until I looked into that little boy's eyes that morning.

I left the house and I sat in a snowbank and I cried and I cried. I returned home about four that afternoon. Barbara was at her mother's house with Tommy. I called her up on the telephone and I said, "Barbara, don't laugh at me, but I think I'm an alcoholic. I need help."

Barbara started going to the seminars with me. The funny thing, we sat in the parking lot for about twenty minutes because there were some people in front of the church where the meeting was to take place. I was afraid they would think I was going to one of those alcoholics' meetings. Of course I'd sit in a bar for twelve hours, and I wouldn't care, but I was ashamed to have anyone see me going to this meeting.

I met the most sensitive people at the seminars. When Lauren died, a friend I met at the meetings spent that night with Barbara and me. Many people came to the hospital.

My group meets on Saturday night. I go sometimes on a lecture tour to speak. Every month Barbara would give me a little cake to celebrate another four weeks without my drinking. Three years have gone by. Barbara doesn't bake the cakes anymore. It's old hat. I'm free.

I loved Barbara, but I couldn't show it in the beginning. I've met many sober alcoholics when I've gone on retreats. Everyone I've talked to always say their whole lives felt as if they were wearing masks and living in fear that the world would see them for what they really are.

I'd like to think I'm a better person, but I think I'm harder on myself now.

Who is to say? Maybe fifteen years from now my son will remember this story. He might go into medicine and deal with children like the sister he almost had. Who knows what Lauren will do?

Remember that movie, *It's a Wonderful Life,* where George discovers what the world would have been like if he had never been born?

The world is different because my daughter lived one day.

Barbara often says that she would have had her tubes tied after Lauren's birth, but now we'd like another baby. If we have another baby, that child will exist because of Lauren.

I've thought a lot about the way things are held together, how one thing seems to work because of something else.

I return again and again to Thomas Merton's last chapter of his book, *New Seeds of Contemplation:*

> The more we persist in misunderstanding the phenomenon of life, the more we analyze them out into strange finalities and complex purposes of our own, the more we involve ourselves in sadness, absurdity and despair. But it does not matter much, because no despair of ours can alter the reality of things, or stain the joy of the cosmic dance which is always there. Indeed, we are in the midst of it, and it is in the midst of us, for it beats in our very blood, whether we want it to or not.
>
> Yet the fact remains that we are invited to forget ourselves on purpose, cast our awful solemnity to the winds and join in the general dance.

Like anybody else I've had troubles, and the routine of living. I have a job. I work every day. I try to do things right.

When Lauren died, I said to myself, "Why bother? Why bother being good? Why bother having kids? Why bother?" Those were the questions going through my mind. "Why did this happen?"

Many times I thought, "If I wasn't me, this wouldn't have happened to my daughter. If I was a better person, this wouldn't have happened."

I don't believe that now.

I feel as if the hurt should go away. I think about her every day. I think about her for about five minutes, then it passes, then I'm O.K. again. I think that she is an angel.

There are plenty of children like Lauren, more than anyone

hears about, but people don't want to talk about that. People don't want to talk about babies dying.

I am amazed at people who won't leave themselves open.

I was trying to tell Barbara the night she cried in a restaurant how much I missed Lauren. I told her how I often think what Lauren would be like, like having her out there on the dock while I'm swimming, spitting water out of my mouth and making Lauren laugh at her daddy. That's never going to happen.

For people to just push those things out of their minds to the point where they are miserable for the rest of their lives, to me it almost makes it an insult to that person who lived, suffered and died. It makes it as if they did all that in vain.

I miss Lauren, but I wouldn't, if Barbara was going to be pregnant again and I knew this was going to happen, I wouldn't wish Barbara not to be pregnant just because this was going to happen.

I don't know what I got out of it. The general dance? It is hard to describe it, but it's just a feeling about things.

*   *   *

One week after I returned from Rhode Island, I received this letter from Lauren's father:

Dear Chris:

Barbara and I want to thank you for coming to see us. I hope you felt at home. Your visit meant so much.

Barbara and I have experienced Lauren's life and death from different perspectives. I can only begin to imagine how Barbara felt when I had to tell her Lauren had died. A mother and child's love is something I can never know. My wife is a wonderful person. She has been a great source of strength for me.

There is something I want to tell you about. I didn't mention it while you were here. From my own point of view, it's the most important thing that's ever happened to me.

Shortly after Lauren was buried I began having dreams, a series of dreams I should say. I was looking, searching for something, but in the dream I didn't know what. It wasn't a nightmare really, but I did feel very anxious. I would bump into boxes, but they weren't what I was looking for. They were too big. And they were stacked up, one on top of the other. I had this dream night after night for about two months.

The last night I had this dream, I bumped into a box again, but this one was different. It wasn't the small one I had been searching for, but I knew somehow I needed to find this one too. In it was my father. I reached up and directly above him was Lauren in the small box I had been looking for. I have not had the dream since.

From the time of the first dream I knew the obvious . . . that in my heart I had not let Lauren go. The small box is, of course, her coffin, but I believe it has another meaning, a much more significant meaning.

Jung often refers to what he termed the "quarternity"—a four-cornered object or image which appeared in the dreams of hundreds of his patients. This "quarternity" was something represented by four candles or a room with four corners—hundreds of variations, but it always had a religious significance pointing toward an inner conflict or search.

As you know, although I was raised a Catholic, I do not attend mass, and theology in general is difficult for me to grasp. I have always believed in God, but his love for me was a "fatherly love"—a love that must be earned and can be taken away. That is what I thought. The Trinity had one element missing—that of "motherly love"—love that is given unconditionally and can never be withdrawn.

When my father died, I felt a great deal of guilt. I loved him very much, but doubted I deserved his love.

The morning I woke after this last dream I was filled with the feeling that he did love me, just as I am. And in the dream Lauren was resting above him. She had brought us together, my father and I. In a sense she had brought me to myself. I was able to feel at peace . . . the power of the powerless.

Most people would think I'm crazy to believe in such things. I am sure that if I had the strength of the Church to call upon, such a dream would not have been necessary. Lacking that, I believe God helped me in another way. I do not pretend to understand such things. If someone tells me they have never had such an experience, all I can say is, "I have."

To me Lauren's life and death made this possible. Because of her, my life and the lives of the people I love are more beautiful. Meeting with you and talking about Lauren is part of that too.

Best wishes,
Peter

There, I thought. After five months I finished Peter's and Barbara's and Tommy's and Lauren's story. Things are a little bit more orderly in the world, I said to myself.

I was pleased with the way Peter's words came out on the page. I wanted to call and tell him on the phone.

"Peter. I finished Lauren's part of the book. I am grateful to you for sharing all that you shared."

And so, a postscript: Peter said with a steady voice, "Barbara is pregnant. She told me Christmas Eve."

That following summer Barbara gave birth to a child . . . a girl . . . Katie.

Chapter VII

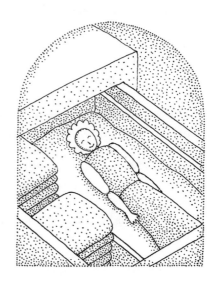

Oliver's room was the second to the left down the hall. His room was always painted in bright yellow. He could not see, but his bedspread was always the one with the greatest number of flowers; the curtains were full, white and clean.

When Oliver outgrew his crib, my father built him a bed which had a high, flat thin board, like a door attached to the side to prevent Oliver from tumbling out, which he never did. To the right of the bed was a white box where we kept his diapers and shirts.

I always liked to drop the lever and open the "door" to Oliver's bed. I liked to sit on the edge. It was a comfortable place. I liked the softness of my brother's limp hand.

Sometimes my mother would experiment with a new food for Oliver, and run something in the blender. If he didn't like the taste of a spoonful of strained peas, he would spit and shower himself, us, the wall with a wide green spray.

There was not any clear reason for the convulsions Oliver endured in the night. I remember waking to the sounds of his deep, guttural gasping for air. I remember my parents running from their bedroom, down the hall and into Oliver's room. I remember being warm in my bed and comfortable and thinking, Well, they'll take care of him. God, that sounds awful. Then I'd go to sleep.

My brothers and sisters and I rarely discussed Oliver. He was, simply, there, a part of us. My sister made him a Christmas stocking one year. She often invited friends to the house and bragged, "We have an angel upstairs. Want to see him?"

It is difficult to explain the hidden reality which is all around us. The poets know how to peel back what we see every day and expose that hidden beauty or truth.

The house where I grew up, the house of Oliver, contained many secrets. The older I became, the more I realized that those secrets weren't as unique as I had once thought they were, but that is the charm of childhood. I once thought the snow fell outside the house just for me, and that the oil delivery man made funny faces for only two children in the world: my sister and me as we watched him wiggle his ears or make clown faces as he waited for our oil tank to fill.

I thought that we were the only family in the world with a brother like Oliver.

Great and small things held great mystery for me when I was a child.

I didn't like dolls. A whistle, a magnifying glass, a pop gun, these were of great value to me when I was eight. Dolls cluttered the steps, slept on my sister's bed during the night, and caused me great misery one afternoon when I tried to apply red, blue and yellow war paint with my crayons onto the cheeks of my sister's Chatty Kathy.

But there was a brief time when I felt an unexplainable attraction for one particular doll.

My mother, who came to this country in 1948, brought with her a large crate filled with furniture, and a number of metal trunks with the bold white letters QUEEN ELIZABETH, NEW YORK, stenciled on their sides. Some were filled with clothes and photographs, others with tablecloths and lace. Deep inside one of these trunks was a porcelain doll my mother had kept since her childhood, a baby doll in a beige nightgown and white bonnet.

Maybe I liked the doll because it belonged to my mother when she was a little girl; maybe it had something to do with the thrill of discovering a small, hidden thing.

Having little to do in the house one afternoon, I went snooping through the dresser that was kept next to Oliver's bed. This oak dresser was used for storing wrapping paper, faded but useful sheets, old photographs and empty boxes.

I pulled open the top right-hand drawer, and lifted a neatly folded collection of monogrammed handkerchiefs my father refused to use, even though my grandfather, a retired general of the Belgian Army, gave them to him on his birthday.

Under these handkerchiefs I discovered this little doll, eight inches long, dressed for bed.

When I picked it up I pulled off the bonnet. I was surprised to feel how cold the doll's head felt. I was not used to handling porcelain. If something wasn't made of plastic, I thought it couldn't be considered a toy.

The doll's eyes moved up and down. Its arms and legs were loose in their sockets. I even held it upside down and noticed how the head and neck moved out of the shoulders just a bit. It was resting in a box without a lid, carefully cushioned in a bed of tissue paper. Its hands were the size of sugar cubes; its feet looked like chips of ivory.

I quickly placed the doll back into the box, covered it up with the handkerchief, and closed the drawer. For weeks I returned to the drawer just to have a look at the doll, just to make sure it was still there, still sleeping on its back with the painted smile on its face. I'd open the drawer to see that its eyes were still peacefully closed, then I felt secure enough to run out and shoot my pop gun.

The older I became the more I realized that there were more things hidden away in the house: the secret compartment in my mother's mahogany desk, the elegant Belgian hunting rifle with a carved handle and engraved barrel wrapped in felt my father kept on top of the living room bookcase. And I was surprised twice by my discovery of an old tuxedo in the attic trunk.

I was surprised the first time because I thought the tuxedo would make the perfect Halloween costume I was desperately looking for that October.

I was surprised the second time by the sad look my father gave me when I ran downstairs dressed for a 1932 ball screaming, "Trick-or-Treat!" That Halloween I collected my candy throughout the neighborhood dressed as a hobo.

Of course, one of the best-kept secrets in our house was kept during the Advent season. I never knew where my parents hid the Christmas presents. I also was never quite sure where they kept the boxes and cookie tins of ornaments and decorations.

At the end of each Christmas season, we unhooked the Christmas bulbs and gold star as my mother carefully wrapped each piece and placed them back into the proper box. I never knew where these boxes were kept during the year, somewhere in the attic of course, but that was too much to imagine, all that color and music and vacations and ice skating and stockings and presents packed away for another twelve months.

So it was with great joy that I saw in mid-December the stacks of Christmas boxes on the dining room table, waiting for the tree to arrive on the roof of my father's white Ford station wagon. The arrival of those boxes was the first real sign that the adults in the house were finally taking Christmas seriously. It was the first indication that soon the house would be transformed: the stockings hung on the fireplace screen, the Christmas cards taped to the door frames, the Christmas embroidery tacked to the mantle, fresh pine boughs draped on the walls, and tables sprinkled with little blue, red and green bulbs my grandmother brought from Belgium one year. But what I liked best about the Christmas decorations in my house when I was eight was the crèche.

My father had the ability to turn ordinary things into things of fancy and magic. I remember the way he'd fold and snip a simple piece of typing paper into acrobatic planes that made wonderful loops and turns on the back lawn. If he made pancakes, he would press the snaking S-design of a kitchen utensil right in the middle. He built my brother and me two castles made from wood, each with its own coat of arms painted about the drawbridge. My father's mastery over the ordinary included our nativity scene.

One of the many Christmas boxes from the attic, the green one shaped in a square, held the painted plaster figures of Joseph and Mary, the orange cow and the gray donkey. The base of one of the three kings was broken. He stood on a piece of clay. A bearded shepherd was on one knee presenting what looked like gold eggs in his upturned hat. The other shepherd had a metal staff which slid up and down in the little hole drilled through his hand. One sheep never stood up, and the other was low, on the ground, with its legs tucked under his white painted wool. The baby Jesus was on his back with his arms extended and his head capped in a halo.

Instead of arranging each figure on a piece of ordinary red cloth on the ordinary dining room table, instead of buying a miniature stable with an angel attached to the peak of the slanting roof, my father created the nativity scene year after year with rocks, moss, sticks, sand and dried grass. He built the crèche upon a large metal pan shaped in a square with a small lip around the edge. Pressed in the center of the pan was a large spoon. As I look back now, I see that the pan was probably a cooking tray that slipped inside the oven, but it was, to me, another of those mysterious objects kept in a closet or in the basement until Christmas.

My sisters and brothers and I were always given the task of gathering moss and sticks and dried grass. My father collected the right-sized rocks which were always kept under the front porch.

As each of us returned to the house, we placed what we found on an old copy of the New York *Times* which was spread out on the living room floor. My mother had already washed the pan and lined it with aluminum foil.

Everything was set.

My father placed three or four rocks in such a way that a small cave was formed. He covered the rocks with moss and dark earth. At the front of the cave, and out upon the complete length of the pan, he spread the dirt smoothly with his long hands. He added some moss and grass here and there, a tree, a mound, a pond. God must have had a great time making the world, I thought, as I watched Bethlehem sprout up on our living room table once again. It was the showpiece of our Christmas decorations. We children made a point of leading all our holiday visitors to the crèche to admire our father's work.

After we cleaned up the remaining dirt and moss and rolled up the newspaper and threw it all away, the final job was to place each figure of the nativity scene in its proper position. My father left that job for us.

It was obvious where Joseph and Mary were to go: in the cave. The three kings were kept off to the side, standing in a row, slightly on an angle. The cow and donkey were always to the left and right of Mary and Joseph. The small wood manger, of course, was placed in the middle of everything. My sister was about to lay the plaster infant in the manger, when my mother said, "Not yet,

Maria. On Christmas Day we can put the baby Jesus in the manger." So my sister respectfully put the infant back in the box.

Each year at this point my sisters, brothers and I would gather around the newly constructed crèche and sing "Oh come, oh come Emmanuel." It was at this particular moment one year that I slowly drew my hand out from under the table, reached into the green box, grabbed the infant Jesus, and slipped him into my pocket without anyone noticing.

"And ransom captive Israel." The song was over.

I knew the small figure belonged in the box until Christmas and not in my whistle-and-dime-filled pocket. I knew I would have to return him to the box so no one would notice that he was missing. What I wasn't really sure about was the reason I took him. Possibly because it was another one of those mysterious things hidden away in the house? Possibly because it was the center of the holiday, and I always wanted to be the center of something in my house of three brothers and two sisters? As we continued to sing other songs, I stared at the empty manger.

"Who wants to decorate the tree?" my mother asked at the end of the final song. It was more of an announcement than it was a question.

I spent the rest of the day hanging ornaments and tinsel, drinking apple juice, darting back and forth from room to room with my brothers and sisters in the eternal game of "Gotcha Last," eternal until my father ordered a recess. Then I rolled under the tree and looked eye to eye with a red Christmas bulb. I liked to see my nose and eyes bulge out toward me in the curve of the ornament. I liked the smell of the tree, the lights spotted throughout the branches.

Alone under the tree, a bit tired, I remembered the baby Jesus deep inside my pocket.

I looked around the living room and felt secure as I saw everyone reading or playing "Chutes and Ladders." I dug into my pocket and felt with my fingertips the edges of a small leg, a little head and one arm . . . One arm? In all the rolling and jumping and running I had done since borrowing the baby Jesus, I must have tumbled on my side which broke off the left arm. I wanted to cry, but I couldn't risk detection.

I slowly pulled the small plaster figure out of my pocket. Not only was his arm severed, but his rubbing again and again against the whistle and dime in my pocket caused deep gashes all about his stomach, face and legs. I pinched around the inside lining of my pocket until I felt the thin rough arm in the very bottom where there was still bits of sand and dirt we had brought in earlier that day.

The baby Jesus was ruined.

Suddenly all the Christmas company, all my brothers and sisters, my father and mother, even Joseph and Mary were not going to be able to stare and admire the center of Christmas. Instead they were all going to wag their fingers in my face. I was always afraid of the three kings, but the idea of having the whole family staring at me in anger was impossible to imagine.

I thrust the broken figure back into my pocket as my father announced from his book, "Time for bed."

The next day would be Christmas. I took the chipped and ruined infant with me to bed. Lying on my back under my covers I tried to imagine what the next day would be like. We will get up much too early, open our stocking gifts, then make enough noise to wake Papa and Mom. They will dress and step into the living room; then Maria will be asked to place the baby Jesus in the crib. We will sing "Joy to the World," and then we will open the presents.

But how, I thought, deep under my covers, could there be presents and songs tomorrow, on Christmas Day without the baby Jesus? Again I wanted to cry, but I was afraid I'd wake everyone up—that is when I remembered the little porcelain doll my mother had hidden in the top right-hand dresser drawer.

The inside covers of my bed were already warm for the night, but I slipped out into the cold darkness of the room. Everything was cold: the doorknob, the walls down the hall, the top of the dresser. Curiously, though, the little porcelain doll felt warm in my hands. I picked it up out of the cardboard box, then I quietly closed the drawer.

"Merry Christmas, Oliver," I whispered to him in the darkness as I closed the door to his room.

It was easy to walk through the house in the shadows, down the stairs, past the front closet, into the living room where the Christmas tree stood. I turned on a lamp. The tinsel on the tree moved back and forth, stirring slightly from the radiators' heat.

The crèche was just as fine and just as ready for the baby Jesus as it was during the day. The night was ready. My sisters and brothers were ready. My mother and father, Joseph and Mary, the world was ready. I picked up a shepherd and a few sticks and placed them a good deal to the right of the nativity. Then I smoothed the earth a bit with my hand and placed the porcelain doll in its beige gown and bonnet before Mary and Joseph's cave. Of course the doll was much too large for the crèche, but that was the best I could do.

I turned off the light. I walked back to my room. The sheets of my bed were still warm, and then I went to sleep quickly, secure with the thought that, once again, the Christmas secret would be safely revealed in the morning.

Chapter VIII

I would not have written the story about Oliver if Tom Lashnits and Diana Schneider of the *Reader's Digest* hadn't asked me to do so so many months before.

I remember as I told them about Oliver's dying, about his fingernails we had to clip, about his "introducing" me to Roe, I remember how these two editors' eyes moistened during our "business" lunch.

They both allowed me to speak. They both listened, asked the right questions. They were the ones who gave me the confidence and the official go-ahead to write about Oliver.

Something wonderful too: After they turned down my manuscript, after *The Wall Street Journal* accepted the article, the editors at the *Reader's Digest* were pleased the piece was so well accepted and asked if, after all, they could publish Oliver's story.

So, I have two reasons why I am grateful to the *Reader's Digest:* (1) They were the ones who asked for Oliver in the first place, and (2) because the *Digest* reprinted my article in the July issue, Nancy Pratico of Hyattsville, Maryland, read about Oliver and wrote me this letter:

Dear Mr. de Vinck:

Thank you so much for taking the time to describe life with your "powerless" brother, Oliver. My family and I were deeply moved by the account that appeared in the July *Reader's Digest.* Our own "Oliver" is named Anthony. He, too, was born in April. He is ten years old and he is my grandson.

His birth was traumatic for all of us. His brain dangled from a hole in his skull that didn't close when it should have during pregnancy. When it became clear he was not going to die immediately from the consequences of that condition, doctors removed the exposed brain, closed the hole, and told us to place him in an institution. Anthony's father—with "only" love and compassion to guide him— brought him home and taught us all about human love.

Ten years ago your article would probably not have created the impact on us that it does today. Since then, like you, we have grown in knowledge by the experience of having Anthony in our lives. It has added a whole new dimension to our understanding of the world and the people in it. Still we have thousands of questions. For example, how much did Oliver grow? How did caring for him change in later years? I suspect that your mom learned how to manage through trial and error as we did. Yet, I wonder if a need exists for some sort of national foundation

and events. "No despair can alter the reality of things, or stain the joy." Children like Oliver, Lauren and Anthony exist as is. We decide if they are to be our tragedies, or if they are to be our triumphs.

Vince, Anthony's father, told me this story with a quiet, strong voice, the voice of a man who chose to define his son as a triumph.

* * *

I remember the doctor saying, as she examined my wife Angie, "Maybe it should be May instead of April."

"No," Angie answered. "I think I'm pretty sure when I got pregnant."

"Well, let's just be sure. I'll have you go to the hospital for some X rays."

Angie thought there was something wrong about two weeks before the baby was due because he wasn't moving.

At the hospital the doctor did a sonogram which didn't turn out that well, so she decided to do an amniocentesis test on the baby. That didn't come out well either. That is when we all knew, for sure, that something was wrong. We didn't know what it was, but we knew something.

Angie was a week away from giving birth, so there wasn't much we could do.

When she finally went into labor, she was quickly admitted to the hospital and hooked up to a fetal monitor. The doctor could tell immediately that the baby was in some distress, but even then no one knew exactly what it was. That is when the doctor elected to do an emergency cesarean because she figured the baby wouldn't survive a regular birth.

Maybe this was nature's way of telling us. Who knows. The doctor came out and said, "Well, we have two choices. We can go ahead and have a regular birth and maybe the baby won't make it, or you could have a C-section."

"We'll have a cesarean and see what happens."

We didn't really know anything about this. For us this was something we never thought about. It was like a bad dream. Here we were waiting for our first baby, and the next thing the doctor and social workers were telling us, "Don't get too attached to the baby after he is born."

They had Angie frightened. They were telling her also, "Don't get attached to the baby because he's not going to live."

Let's face it. This was the first time we had ever experienced something like this. We figured these people were experts. They're supposed to know, so we tried not to get attached to the baby.

When the baby was born his head was in the shape of a little cone and part of his brain was hanging out of his skull. They call it hernia of the brain. The best the doctors could do was to cut off that part of the exposed brain and sew up the open skull.

We were told that babies like this might last a week or two, but eventually infection would set in and that would be it. He looked like such a muscular kid when he was born, but everyone kept telling us, "Don't get attached. The baby won't survive."

My wife was in intensive care, and the baby was in an incubator with that strange, ugly head. Then my sister, Mimma, came up right after the birth, right after the first shock. This, I later saw, was the turning point for me.

Mimma was standing there looking at this strange baby through the glass of the incubator, and all she said was, "All that baby needs is some love." That's really all she said. "All that kid needs is love."

I really didn't hear what she said then. It didn't sink in. After all, everybody was telling me not to get attached.

My mother-in-law Nancy remembers. She said she was getting so successful at getting unattached during the next few days that when she heard the nurses say, "It's time to feed Anthony," she was taken aback.

"They're calling him a *name?*" Nancy said. "They're calling him by his *name?* You mean that's really a person?"

Nancy said that she just kept calling him "the baby," or she kept thinking of it as just an object. When she heard the nurses say, "Anthony," she was really taken aback. That stayed in her mind. "They are calling him Anthony. Right."

During that same time I came home from the hospital one evening and casually said to Nancy, "Well, Anthony was cooing a bit."

"Cooing!" Nancy called out. "Cooing! You mean he was cooing? He makes noises?"

"Yes," I said. She was startled. This was a human being. That's how successful Nancy, Anthony's grandmother, was at turning him out of her heart. But that all changed when we all stopped listening to the professional advice and started listening to Anthony.

My philosophy all along was that I didn't care how long Anthony would live. He was going to know the embrace of his father's and mother's arms.

During Anthony's first three months of life, he had to undergo a number of operations. Many times the hospital called to say Anthony had a bad day; he probably won't live. And still there was that suggestion that we not get attached. The baby won't survive.

I guess people, if it is not their own child, really don't know. It is easy for me to tell you this is good or not good for you, but how do people know how I or Angie feel about things inside.

They kept changing his bandages and feeding him in the hospital, then we really started seeing changes in Anthony. He was big enough to smile and giggle a bit, and this is when we decided, to heck with it. We're going to bring him home.

Many people said to my wife and me, "How can you live like this? How can you live knowing what Anthony is going to be like?"

But Angie and I decided, "Look. Who knows who is going to die first? It isn't that he is going to die first."

I don't know. Who knows. I could walk out of the door and get killed by a car. We decided that as long as we had Anthony, we were going to give him as much as we could. Every day that we have him, that's it. As long as we can take care of him at home, we don't have any problems. This is it.

When we stopped trying to do anything with Anthony, that is, when we gave up trying to put him in an institution, when we stopped trying to make him something he wasn't, when we stopped trying to do other than accept him and bring him love, we brought Anthony home, relaxed, and said, "This is it. We can now take one day at a time."

We had a long discussion saying if things didn't work out, we'd try something else. My biggest concern was leaving Angie home alone with Anthony. What if the baby died when she was by herself? I wouldn't like that.

I remember the first night we brought Anthony home. Angie and I didn't sleep at all. For a long time he didn't sleep. If he was crying, we didn't know why. We didn't know what to do. We didn't know if something was causing him trouble, if he might die, or if he was just hungry or awake. We didn't know.

Anthony was in pain a great deal during those earlier years. In the beginning we couldn't interpret what his problems were. Now, if he cries one way, we know. If he cries another way we know what that means too. He gets seizures. That we know too. Sometimes there is nothing we can do. We just leave him in a chair and he'll cry maybe fifteen, twenty minutes. We know he goes through this and eventually he'll relax.

There were times in the beginning when we first brought Anthony home when it was not easy. Only now, the past two years, have things become normal.

Many times I thought back then that it would be better if

something happened, if Anthony died. I never think that anymore. I hold him a lot.

It got easier caring for Anthony the older he got, once we learned what made him do certain things.

He gets Angie and me motivated. We do more to try and help him out. We see what he needs. We need him.

Lots of times Anthony has to burp, so we get him some baking soda. Many times he wants to sleep.

Sometimes when I come home late from work, this little rascal is still awake. I'll say, "Are you waiting for me, Anthony?" Of course he never responds, but I'll give him a few kisses and then he'll go to sleep.

Many times he'll be moaning and we'll be in bed. Angie will say, "Well, Anthony wants to come in with us." She picks him up and brings him to bed. He loves to lie in bed with us. Two minutes he's sleeping.

Many times when we pick him up, he smiles, like a sigh of relief. If he needs help with something, maybe a burp, he will give this big sigh when it is over, and we'll know everything is all right.

Many times Anthony will cry in the middle of the night. We just go to him, roll him to another position, and boom, he's asleep again. We like to watch him sleep.

We learned little tricks. We'd pat his nose and Anthony would laugh. It is a series of magical little discoveries.

We brought him home for the first time on December ninth. We always said that we'd call December ninth Anthony's birthday because that is the day we brought him home with us. April thirtieth is his real birthday, but his life began in a real way on the day we took him home.

That first Christmas was special. Christmas is for kids. We bought a tree and decorations, even though we knew Anthony wasn't much aware of it all. We just acted like he was with us more than he was.

My family, my wife, our parents, we all thought at first that we weren't so great after all. We always thought we were special, not like anyone else. Then Anthony was born. We couldn't understand how something like this could happen to us. Who are we, we thought, to think we're so great that this shouldn't happen to us?

We used to have council meetings with the family around the kitchen table when all this began. It wasn't easy in the beginning. We'd sit and be a mini-support group. We'd just sit, I remember for hours, depending on what crisis was coming up at the time and just talk it all out.

The organized support groups are terrific too. When he was born I thought we were the only ones with a boy like Anthony. Then we met other people, and we'd compare and say, "Oh yes, Anthony does that too." Those support groups helped.

I never had any guilty feelings. Many social workers would say, "You and your wife seem like you have your heads on because you don't seem to need our help."

I remember one social worker said, "Is there anything you want to discuss? How are things at home?"

I said, "Fine. We are taking it day by day."

"That is marvelous. I have so many parents who are falling apart."

"Believe me," I quickly answered. "We've had our moments where we would just cry. We'd just sit there and cry."

One of the first glorious days was on a Sunday. Angie was giving Anthony a bottle and burping him, and then he made his first noise, then he started smiling. That was a big turnover.

I remember, too, when he first started giggling. Angie said he was in his crib. She was in the kitchen cooking while I was on my way home from work.

It was around six o'clock. Angie said she was cooking in the kitchen when suddenly she just heard this giggling in the next room. Just giggling. This laughing. I don't know. Angie couldn't wait until I came home. "Vince," she said, "you won't believe it, but Anthony just started giggling." Then he giggled for me. He still does it. Just giggling.

Anthony is just like Oliver. People would call him a vegetable too.

Many times, even today, especially on his birthday, we look down at him sitting in his chair. He's so small. His tenth birthday was traumatic. Anthony has already surprised the doctors. They said he wouldn't live. He's been baptized twice: once when he was born because he wasn't supposed to make it, and once here, across the street at St. Jerome's.

When Anthony was first born, I was looking at other kids and I was really jealous and mad. We were having dinner one day with the family, and I saw all the children, my niece Franchesca in particular. She was one year old. She was beginning to talk and walk. Everybody was making a big fuss about her. I was angry. That was a Sunday, and just before I had to go to the hospital to see Anthony, I watched everyone playing with Franchesca. I even said, "Hey, look! Look at that. She can eat spaghetti." But somehow this all made me feel so much closer to Anthony.

Even today I take Anthony with me to his brother's baseball games and I think sometimes, as I watch my other son, Michael, that Anthony has been cheated out of all that. I watch all the boys running the bases, calling out the names of their friends. I think Anthony will never be able to do that. But of course there are many other things we see in Anthony that the other kids don't have.

My concerns are never about my own children's reactions to Anthony, but what other children think. There are some kids in school sometimes who, well, Michael says they say bad things about Anthony. A couple of times Michael says someone made a face or pointed a finger. It is generally the children we don't know, but the majority of the kids come and say, "Oh he's cute."

My daughter Christine said that when someone came up and

stared, she looked him in the eye and said, "Who you lookin' at?" She protects Anthony.

One night I got home late from work, around ten-thirty. I took a shower, then I went to the television and watched the football game for a while. I saw a light under Anthony's bedroom door. I said to myself, "Gee. Angie must be up with Anthony." So I walked upstairs, and there I saw Christine sleeping right next to Anthony.

She'll do this many times. If we check her room and she's not there, she's sleeping next to her brother. It might be her motherly instincts, the nurturing. Christine changes Anthony's diapers and brings Anthony downstairs for us. She feeds him, pats his nose, sings to him.

One year Michael brought home bells for Anthony for Christmas.

Anthony is generally happy. It's been a long time since he's cried. We take him outside. He likes sitting in the sun, the warm sun against his skin. He likes that.

He sleeps in his own bed. He has his own chest of drawers, a little wicker chair. We lay him on his side. He seems to like that position. It's better if you hold him so he's not so floppy. Considering what he's been through, he's very healthy. He doesn't give us much trouble at all.

A casual observer won't notice anything about Anthony. They'll say, "Oh, he's sleeping." Sometimes they'll say, "How old is he?" When we say ten, their eyes get all big and wondering. He hasn't grown much. He is about twenty-four pounds.

We like the routine. Angie says when Anthony comes home from school she is happy to just get to hold him. If the radio is on she loves to hold Anthony on her lap and jump him up and down with the music. He loves music. He just responds to the music and the bouncing.

Sometimes Anthony is not doing so well. What I love to do, he loves to bite, so I give him my finger wrapped in a cloth so he doesn't hurt me, and that stops his crying. He becomes calm. As soon as he does that, he's fine.

The way Anthony is, I would say that he moves us to action. We have this child, and in a way we do more in our lives to help him out. *We* see a need for him.

Before Anthony was born I had a business. I still do: two successful restaurants. Before Anthony was born things used to bother me more, little things. Something with the business. I'd really get down and it would get to me, but since Anthony, my attitude toward life is so different you wouldn't believe it.

There is nothing that is going to bother me, especially if I can't control it.

We survived. Anthony, the way he is, made me a better man. I enjoy my life a little bit more. I see things.

This little guy did that. I think so. There's no doubt about that. If Anthony hadn't been born the way he is, who knows, maybe I'd have ulcers by now, lost my hair or something.

Anthony has brought us a special joy. There are many headaches, but let's face it, sure, we're going to have a few more headaches than most people, but when our son smiles, when he giggles, that makes it all worthwhile.

The business that I have has many problems, but I never let them bother me. I just do the best I can, then I come home to Angie, Christine, Michael, and I come home to Anthony.

Chapter IX

Three years before my brother died, my mother wrote an article for *Sign* magazine about Oliver, about discovering the exact nature of his condition when he was a child. She wrote about those hidden joys which were waiting to be discovered in the mystery of suffering.

*   *   *

It's hard to express what such a verdict means to a mother. It pierced me to my depth, ripped apart the very fabric of life when we discovered how severely different Oliver was going to be all his life. It was not something one could put aside or escape. The world appeared darkened: It was as if the whole of reality had been covered with a gray film. I didn't understand yet.

By the grace of God (and I don't use this as a figure of speech), I could accept it, in darkness and ignorance—yes, even manage a simple, immediate consent. I remember holding Oliver and saying the Lord's Prayer, over and over: "Thy will be done on earth as it is in heaven." I could not see the purpose of this trial, but I could say yes to God. I could begin to learn about trust, could begin to realize that God's ways are not our ways.

For many, many years, I was confined to the house, alone and without the support of relatives or friends. José was at work all day and I was with Oliver and the other five children. This enforced seclusion was difficult for me; I had a restless, seeking spirit. Through Oliver, I was held still. I was forced to embrace a silence and a solitude where I could "prepare the way of the Lord." Sorrow opened my heart, and I "died." I underwent this "death" unaware that it was a trial by fire from which I would rise renewed—more powerfully, more consciously alive.

I looked into the abyss of human sorrow and saw how dangerous and how easy it is to slide into self-pity—to weep over one's fate. I was given the grace to understand that one has to be on guard against such grieving, for it falsifies one's grasp on life and erodes one's inner strength. Sorrow can be worn as a badge of honor ("See how I suffer!"). It can also be a searing experience. It is not exalting to be alone all day in a house full of small children, to be faced with the same daily chores, with a routine of physical work which appears to narrow one's life to trivial concerns. Many women who are "just housewives" experience this sense of futility, this feeling of being cut off from the mainstream of life.

But if there is a silence that is opaque and a solitude that is a prison, there is also a silence that is luminous and a solitude that is blessed terrain where the seeds of prayer can grow.

When Oliver was a baby, an event took place that illustrates the spiritual dimension this child brought into our lives. In one of the great cathedrals of Europe, a special benediction for the sick had been planned. At the time, we were living nearby, so we decided to bring Oliver to the service.

All the chairs and pews had been removed from the church. The nave and aisles were filled with people in wheelchairs or on stretchers—a very sad and poignant sight. The Blessed Sacrament was carried through the church, elevated in blessing. When the procession stopped close to where we were and the Eucharist was lifted in benediction, a prayer rose from my heart. It was so strong that I was unable to go against it: It asked only "that this child may always remain pure of heart." My whole being was aching to ask that Oliver be healed, for I knew that Jesus of Nazareth was passing by, and my child and I were in need. But I stood there, transfixed, able to pray only for purity of heart.

Over the years I can say that there was not a drop of pain for me left in Oliver's reality. He did not change much. He grew to the size of a ten-year-old child. His hands and feet were those of a five-year-old, but he had a thick beard that had to be shaved. He never left his bed. He lay on his back, unable to lift his head, unable to speak, unable to learn anything.

Oliver was always a "hopeless" case, yet he was such a precious gift for our whole family. "God has chosen the foolish things of the world to confound the wise; and God has chosen the weak things of the world to confound the things which are mighty." (1 Cor 1:27) This child had no *apparent* usefulness or meaning, and the "world" would reject him as an unproductive burden. But he was a holy innocent, a child of light.

Looking at him, I saw the power of powerlessness. His total helplessness speaks to our deepest hearts, calls us not merely to pious emotions but to service. Through this child, I felt bound to Christ crucified—yes, and also to all those who suffer in the world. While caring for Oliver, I also felt that I ministered, in some mysterious way, to all my unknown brothers and sisters who were, and are, grieving and in pain throughout the world. So, through Oliver, I learned the deepest meaning of compassion.

I have made my peace with the coming of Oliver's death. I cannot see it as a tragedy. I know that the child who lived in apparent void and darkness sees God, lives forever in health, beauty and light. Here on earth, he was loved. His presence among us was a mysterious sign of that peace the world cannot give.

Chapter
X

I knew there was a mystery about my house, something beyond Christmas, and dolls, something beyond swinging from the top of pine trees. There was a mystery beyond my climbing between the two walls, a mystery beyond the windows painted shut.

Somehow the peace my parents learned from Oliver was placed on my own heart. Children do what adults do. If parents smoke cigarettes, their children often wind up smoking. If parents are readers, there is a good chance that their children will grow into the reading habit. If parents embrace the enchantments of the heart, there is a good chance their children, too, will laugh. Life imitates life. My parents were able to look at the ordinary and see the extraordinary. I learned to appreciate the sound of water slapping against itself because my father, each spring, took an iron rake and walked to the small stream which divided our property in two. Each spring he pulled sticks, rotting leaves and stones up from the water which broke free the flow of the stream. "Christopher. Listen to the water rushing." So I listened.

I loved the sound of geese because my mother would push back the window: "Children. Listen."

I loved the sound of my mother singing "Silent Night." The more a parent points out things to her children, the more the children will take it upon themselves to select, identify, listen to, see, embrace.

Oliver sharpened my parents' vision. That vision was passed along to me. This is what it was like living in the house of Oliver.

When I was eight, there was much talk about ghosts and dragons. My older brother taught me how to throw a pebble into the air as a bat flew through the fading light of a summer's evening.

"If you throw it ahead of the bat, you can see him swoop down with his radar, catch the rock, and fly off."

The squirrels ran and rattled between the walls of our house. The wind pressed a low wheezing sound through the weather stripping against the front door, and I was at the age where a dare, taking a risk, was a serious matter.

"I dare you to make a mustard sandwich and eat the whole thing." I did.

"I dare you to jump off the garage roof." I did that too.

"I dare you to walk through the woods tonight to the other side and touch the barbed wire fence." That I wasn't so quick to do. After all, I was only eight, and I didn't even have enough courage to walk down into the basement alone with the lights on.

"All you have to do is run through the woods and touch the fence."

"Can I take a flashlight?"

"Nope. That's not part of the dare."

"Can I do it tomorrow morning?"

"Chrissy!"

"Will you come with me?"

"Well, O.K.," my brother said, "but you have to walk all the way to the fence."

Walking out into the dark, even with my older brother, didn't diminish the fear. The snakes were out, and certainly the barking dogs. We had to pass the place where we had buried Tigerlily, my sister's great tomcat who had been hit by a car that winter before.

I began to believe in pirates and kidnappers as my brother and I approached the woods' edge.

"Are you chicken?" he asked.

Of course I wanted to say yes indeed I was chicken, but boys of eight don't like to admit such things. After all, a dare was a dare which had to play itself out as my brother pushed back a low branch and we stepped into the woods.

The dark had, for me, the power to change the shapes and attitudes of things. Trees became giants with drooping beards; the skunk cabbage looked like dinosaur scales. I was about to lose my courage when my brother called out, "Chrissy! Look! Glowing wood!"

I didn't know anything about chemistry or about the reaction certain elements have when exposed to moist air. All I remember was the excitement in my brother's voice and the dim green luminescence.

My brother leaned over an old rotting log as I crouched down on my legs and looked at the small bits of light which clung to the side of the wood.

"Are they bugs?" I asked.

"Nah," my brother answered as he poked one or two flecks of light with his index finger. "It's phosphorescence. My science teacher said so."

I didn't know anything about science either, but I knew this discovery was something to shout about, though the wind and the dark kept me still as I drew my arms around my knees.

"I think it's wonderful," I whispered.

My brother held the end of the log in his right hand, then he slowly twisted the wood around, which revealed, on its belly, a speckled treasure of light, like a galaxy of little stars in the great distance.

"Let's tell Daddy," I said.

"Let's put the log back and maybe we can see the lights again tomorrow."

After my brother carefully placed the log down in its original place, he stood up and I stood up, then he took my hand and we both walked home through the dark as the skunk cabbage brushed against our legs. We both forgot about the dare.

An eye for the spectacular was created in my youth. That vision was enhanced by Oliver's blindness. All that he could not see became, for me, spectacular objects: the carved apples on the legs of the living room table, mushrooms, keys, ferns, bark, pebbles, the moon.

I was brought up in a house where the extraordinary was always discovered in the ordinary. Often, in that discovery, there was a risk.

I can easily explain why I took certain risks as a child: I flung myself off the swing because I wanted to be like the big kids; I smacked the burning cigarette from Ira's hand—a big tough kid in my eighth grade—because I wanted to save him from cancer. Those risks are clear to me, but I cannot explain why I crawled deep inside the honeysuckle to bait the tractor.

That spring the man on the farm behind our house pulled several round disks behind his steaming, clanking tractor.

For some reason, I ran down the lawn, through the woods (it was in the late morning) to the fence which separated our trees from his flat field. Pouring over the fence was a thick green mass of honeysuckle vines fresh in bloom.

I crept to the fence without the farmer seeing me as he plowed his field back and forth; then I crawled deep inside the tangled leaves.

I could see the driver turn his tractor on the far side of the field. I could hear the engine huffing and huffing through its labor; then I waited.

Slowly, as I had expected, the farmer turned toward my direction. The plow cut deep furrows into the earth, closer and closer.

I knew he would have to turn his machine. I knew he would not crash through the fence against the vines, against me hidden like a fetus under the leaves, but I still considered jumping up with outstretched arms, pleading, "Don't run me over!"

I remember the sticks scratching my face, the smell of honeysuckle, the curved red nose of the tractor bearing down on me.

I remember the driver: brown wrinkled skin, his head turning to the right and then to the left as he checked the plow. I could nearly touch him. I was eight. I nearly screamed. Nearly. Nearly, until the man pulled on the black wheel once, twice, as the tractor swung back to the field like a dog who had lost the scent. Clack. Clack. Clack. Clack.

I crawled out of my hiding place, brushed the dirt from my pants, then I ran home. I took the risk. I was triumphant.

Children live with risks, imagine they live in a world of safety surrounded by blurred images, loud voices and monsters. I was no different, especially when someone in the neighborhood would shout, "Zorro is loose!"

To me, Zorro, the neighbor's black dog, had one purpose in life: to bite me. My brothers and sisters probably nurtured that fear by their teasing. No matter. I remember running inside the house and closing the front door behind me whenever I heard, once again, that Zorro had broken his chain.

Then someone, my sister perhaps, whispered, "I dare you to run outside, down the driveway, around the rhododendrons, and back into the house."

I looked at her, a girl. I looked out the front window. I saw the driveway, the trees, the grass; then I pulled the door open, ran down the front stairs, pressed my feet against the stones and leaves. Just as I spun around the rhododendrons and onto the lawn, I heard a loud barking and I saw Zorro leap out from the bushes.

I thought, at the time, that I could run faster than anyone or any thing, even Zorro, until I slipped on the grass and fell. That was the second time in my life I was held by fear. The first was when I was much younger and I woke in the middle of the night with such a nightmare that I couldn't move or call out for help.

Then Zorro barked again. I stood up and ran and ran until I was again safely inside the house against the door.

While I ate mustard sandwiches, while I stood over the glowing wood, while I flirted with tractors and wild dogs, Oliver was on his back, blind, silent, season after season. I thought about that when I was eight.

Today, with courage, I spend my turn with silence, alone writing in my small room down in the basement beside the furnace, as I hear Roe walking and the children rolling marbles upon the wood floor above me.

Often, when the oil burner clicks on with a loud whoosh, I jump in my chair.

There are shadows in the universe, some real, most imagined. When the moon is up, and the air moist, risk a walk alone. What will you gain? The sounds of the dogs barking. The smell of honeysuckle.

Seek out the glowing wood, for it is here, between the soft light and the darkness, you can measure out your true net worth. My brother Oliver in his silence taught me that.

Chapter XI

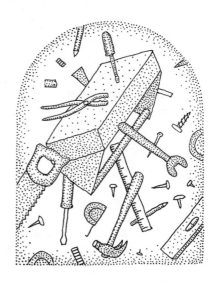

Dear Mr. de Vinck:

I don't know why I started reading this story in *Reader's Digest.* Perhaps it was because of the similarity between Oliver's face and features in the photograph and that of my own fifteen-month-old son, Michael.

Perhaps I should say that before I read your article I was severely depressed and was even considering suicide. I have been chronically unemployed and underemployed for four years and on and off welfare. My wife and I were getting along less and less, and divorce seemed near.

My ex-wife constantly battled with me over my rights as a noncustodial parent. Money problems were constant.

Anyway, as I got halfway through the story about your brother, I suddenly broke down and wept, something I had been unable to do despite my problems.

I don't know if I cried for Oliver or for myself, or for both of us, but the article brought on some serious thinking. I finished reading the story, and then I discussed it with my wife. It seemed to make our problems so trivial. It restored new confidence in myself. I feel so much better. I have new courage to face these things . . . maybe I should say "power" instead of courage. It's really amazing how Oliver can still be so powerful.

Sincerely,
John Fullman (pseudonym)
The West Coast

There must have been reasons for Oliver's birth. Anthony must be part of a plan. The exact moment of Lauren's birth, and the exact moment of Lauren's death must fit between the movement of time. If there are any plans in the universe at all, if there are any patterns, surely they can be discovered mysteriously in the lives of these children.

Because of Oliver, a man from the West Coast began to see new hope, a new power in himself. Much of what we believe in our hearts is proved with hints of certitude: love, compassion, eternity, all hidden in the words we speak, in the gestures we make, in the cycles of the moon.

We will never know exactly what impact each of us will make in the history of our collective human existence, but surely Oliver, Lauren, Anthony are worth more than flies to be slapped away. John Fullman also recognized in himself that he, too, is worth more. All that the poets ask us to do is to *see*. All my mother and father asked us children to do was to *see*. It is our choice as creatures with free will to decide if we are going to see or not see. John Fullman, with the help of Oliver, chose to *see.*

*   *   *

I was famous at getting drunk at someone. Somebody would do something and I'd say to myself, I'll show him. I'll get drunk. I would do that as an attention getter. Poor John is getting drunk.

I finally came to realize that nobody cared. Today I don't want my children to grow up with bad memories of me. I hated my childhood.

My mother was a manipulative person and was always seeking power somehow, and I didn't realize that for years and years. I was an only child for ten years. When my sister came along, my parents were in their thirties. I remember the very first day. I rushed home from school to see my baby sister. I ran through the door full of excitement. "Where is she? Where is she?"

"Shhh! Don't wake her!" It seemed from that day on, John was number two. It was hard for me to adjust. What I didn't know was that my dad felt the same way about me. For years he felt that he was number two after I was born.

Later, when I was a teenager, I remember my parents having violent, terrible arguments. They'd punch each other. My dad pulled a gun on my mom once.

I was caught in the middle of one of their arguments once. I was very young, five or six perhaps. I had just gotten up from a nap. My mom had to go to the store and buy milk. When she returned, my face was all red. My dad slapped me. I was screaming and crying. He took a lot of his frustrations about my mother out on me. My father never had time for me.

When my mom was on one of her suicidal binges, my father would make me stay home from school to keep an eye on her. He always said that someone had to earn the money to keep the insurance going.

I remember once she sent me to the liquor store to buy some razor blades. Here we go again, I thought. I walked down to the store and I called my dad.

"She sent me down here to get some razor blades. What do you want me to do?"

My dad said, "What do you want me to do? I'm working out here."

I hung up the telephone and I walked back home. My mother said, "All right. You go to the park."

I was surprised. I used to have to beg her for permission to go there.

"You go to the park and come back in an hour."

So I went, but I decided to return sooner than she had said. All the doors to the house were locked. The windows were locked. She had locked herself in the kitchen and turned the gas up on the stove. I'll never forget this as long as I live. I thought, Maybe I should let her commit suicide. I could do it. I had been through so much horror already. I was still so immature, but I was smart enough to know that I could get away with a lot of things. But I said, "Naw, I better get her out."

I went into the garage and got a screwdriver and picked the lock of the front door. She was on the floor. She was full of pills. That was her M.O. She had tried to kill herself the night before. I pulled her out of the house. She was taken to the hospital by ambulance. I don't remember much after that. She'd done this so often.

I told my mother years later about what I thought about doing when I first saw her there on the floor. She said, "You wouldn't have had the guts."

I used to hang out with the McMannis family. Irish Catholics. They didn't have anything. They were very poor, but I hung out over there and I liked it. They were a happy family. They had something. Love maybe.

My mother despised the two brothers I hung out with. One was a year older, and one was a year younger than I was. She didn't like them because they were so poor. She hated everybody, and I don't know how she got that way.

She was born during the Depression on one of those dust bowl farms. I guess she just decided that she wasn't going to be poor, and anybody who was could just be damned. I was the same way for a long, long time.

I remember one specific time when I went through boot camp. My dad shook my hand the night I went and said, "You'll be back in two weeks. You'll never make it in the Marines."

After boot camp they sent me to infantry training where I learned how to use a weapon, but I wasn't treated like I thought I should have been. I had to go on guard duty for two weeks. I was so disappointed. I had to walk a post every other hour. I'd sleep in between. I'd be harassed. This went on for about a week when I finally called my mom. I just cried my eyes out and she was real soothing. She said, "Just hang in there. It's only going to last a couple of weeks. You can do it." That was the most tender moment I remember between my mother and me.

Today my motivation is my children. I don't want them to go out into the world emotionally crippled like I was. I was cynical. I was kicked around a lot, and I kicked a lot of people around too.

I spent most of my adult life incoherent. I started drinking when I was seventeen. I didn't really start hitting hard until I was twenty-five.

The biggest disappointment for me was not having been accepted as a hero when I came back from Vietnam. Even my dad told me that he fought in a real war. That broke my heart. I made up all kinds of combat stories to tell my dad. I lied to him. To this day I haven't told him. I don't have the heart to tell him.

When I arrived home I didn't get three steps from the airport when some girl walked up and spit on me. I was wearing my uniform and she spit on me.

I was broke. I had to hitchhike home from the airport. I walked out to the corner. I thumbed and thumbed. Nobody picked me up. Finally, this guy in a crewcut pulled up.

"Get in. Where're you going?"

"Home," I said. "About three miles ahead."

"Well, I'm not going that far, but I'll take you there."

He drove me right to my front door. I had to stand out there all those hours until I got one ride. He was a former Marine. He served in Korea.

Nobody accepted me. My friends even told me I was a fool. My parents' attitude was, "Well, you guys were losing over there."

I'm a blue collar worker today, which is O.K. I am making good money now which helps. I got out of aviation about six years ago, and with the recession I couldn't get back in. They just took the cream of the crop. I had a bad attendance record. They knew I drank. The last place I worked I picked up a coworker's toolbox and threw it about thirty feet because I was angry at him. He worked the other shift. He worked nights and I worked days. We ran the same machine. Every morning when I would come in, the machine would be all screwed up. It would take me a long time to set it up, instead of just putting the part in and running it. I complained. I went to the union. I went to the manager, but nothing was getting done. I went in on the last day before a vacation was about to begin, and there was my machine in its usual useless mess. This guy also kept moving my toolbox all around. I left a note on the box which said, "If you move my toolbox again, I will break your arm." That was it. I had had it.

I came in the next morning, and this guy said, "Did you leave this note on the box?"

I said, "Yes."

"You can't do that," he smirked.

So again I went through the channels. I went back through the union. I went to management. Nothing happened.

Then I got word that I might get fired. That set me off. Fire *me?* I went nuts. I walked down to my machine, and there was this guy's toolbox where mine usually was. I picked up that thing and threw it over the high platform where I was stationed. I hit a steel beam dead center. The box flew open and tools scattered everywhere. I walked out of the job. Big mistake.

It took me a long time to get to where I am today. I was feeling really badly when I read about Oliver. I was seriously contemplating suicide. My wife and I had been on welfare for so long. I started one of those job-training programs, then I ran out of money to support even that. No job. The drinking. The fights. My mother's memory. I was so depressed.

It was a miracle that I opened up that particular story in the magazine that day.

My wife buys the *Reader's Digest* occasionally. When I started reading this part, "We'd wrap a box of baby cereal for Oliver at Christmas and place it under the tree. We'd pat his head with a damp cloth in the middle of a July heat wave. His baptismal certificate hung on the wall. A bishop came to the house and confirmed him."

And the very next line: "Five years after his death Oliver still remains the weakest, most helpless human being I ever met, and yet he was one of the most powerful human beings I ever met. He could do absolutely nothing except breathe, sleep, eat, and yet he was responsible for action, love, courage, insight."

I don't know what it was, but the thought of Oliver living all those years, being in the condition that he was in just made my problems seem so minuscule. I think that is why I cried when I first read the article. I cried for him, and I cried for me. I felt guilty for feeling sorry for myself.

Today I always tell my children, "I don't care if you love me, but when you grow up, you are going to realize that dad wasn't such a bad guy after all."

Because I read about Oliver, I stopped drinking. I don't know really how to explain it. I was mesmerized by the story. I read it over and over and over. Things were starting to formulate in my head. I started to get my determination up I guess.

Then my wife and I started having real good luck. I found this job working in the jet-plane factory, which I still have. I began being honest with people for the first time in many years. I kept rereading about Oliver. I kept reminding myself who he was.

I don't really know how to explain it.

Chapter XII

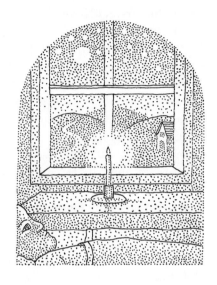

My childhood was interspersed with certain moments which have become the pageantry of my imagination: a porcelain doll hidden in a top drawer, Oliver's cloth diapers spread wide and flat upon the lawns of summer, the glowing wood, the sound of a distant tractor.

I lived beside the mystery of Oliver and I lived through the mystery of childhood. What I didn't realize was that the sense of wonder and peace surrounding those hidden things could be transported beyond the memories I hold of a certain house during a certain time when the geese spoke to me, and the passing days were measured against the laughter of my mother.

I realized that what I learned as a child could be translated so that others could hear the sound of goodness. I realized all this when Oliver's story created such an extraordinary response in the country.

Oliver, Anthony, Lauren, John: relatives to a greater heritage. The phenomenon of life. Oh, Mr. de Vinck. You mean he was a vegetable? Which girl would you marry? I remember the sound of the spoon clicking and ticking against the red plum pudding bowl. I remember the sounds of his convulsions.

"God has chosen the weak things of the world to confound the things which are mighty." Holy innocent. A child of light.

The Christophers in New York City always remind us that, "It is better to light one candle than to curse the darkness." My parents chose to light a candle. Vince and his wife lit a candle. Peter and his wife, John and his wife, they all lit candles.

They say that the Great Wall of China is the only man-made object visible to the astronauts as they revolve around the earth.

What man-made flame of light could we reflect back into the darkness of space if we took up the example of these people who chose to rise out of the ashes and light those candles one by one?

The Christophers also believe that everyone is unique, and that everyone can make a significant contribution to the world. The director of The Christophers, the Reverend John T. Catoir, is our closest family friend. I am inclined to call him Father John T. Catoir-de Vinck. I call him my fourth brother. Father John has been a part of my parents' lives, a part of my brothers' and sisters' lives, a part of my life for twenty years. He has been with us on all the holidays, vacations, joys and sorrows.

Father John married Roe and me, baptized our children, helped us in many of our times of need.

Two days after Oliver died, Father John said the funeral mass and delivered this homily:

"What you did for the least of my brethren you did for me."

Oliver was certainly the least of the brethren; in that sense he was a Christ figure. He was like us in all things but sin. Jesus said, "Learn of me for I am meek and humble of heart." There is much we can learn from the meekness of Oliver. All of us have learned different things from him.

I learned a great deal from him about the power of poverty. Oliver didn't own anything. Just his bed, his box of diapers, a few bottles of medicine. His life and his poverty reminded me of Tolstoy's short story "What Men Live By." In a world where money and possessions are regarded as the only security, Oliver's life gave testimony to the truth that men live by *love*, not possessions. In his poverty, Oliver was rich. He was fortunate enough to be born into a loving family. This is a world where life is not revered. There were an estimated forty million abortions performed in the world last year. Those are the ones that were reported. Oliver was blessed with parents who regarded life as a priceless gift, a sacred trust. Oliver had nothing, but he was immensely rich because of the love that surrounded him.

He would have been thirty-three next month; and though his back never left his sheets, he died with no bedsores. He outlived at least two of the doctors who said that he would surely die before he was five, and then eight, and then twelve. They didn't count on Oliver's devoted parents.

Oliver also taught me about service, the deeper meaning of it. He taught me that we serve not only when we do things for others.

Oliver was never able to do anything in that sense of the word. He was virtually paralyzed, but still he did so much for each one of us. He evoked the best love that was in us. He helped us to grow in the virtues of devotion, wisdom, perseverance, kindness, patience and fidelity. Without doing anything, Oliver made all of us better human beings. He taught us that the importance of service is not exclusively in doing for others but in allowing them to do for us. The meek and humble of heart do all of us a service when they call us to respond in love. For Jesus said, "What you did for the least of the brothers, you did for Me."

Oliver also taught me about innocence. He was never jealous, resentful, he was never deceitful; he never hurt anyone. He kept all the commandments. He never complained. Even during the last four feverish weeks of his life, in spite of visits from two doctors prescribing four different kinds of antibiotics, he did not complain. He was restless at times, unable to overcome the raging fever. He expressed his displeasure at the taste of his medicine, he showed signs of anguish at times, but he was peaceful, calm and silent throughout. He kept all the commandments. But when it came to the third, "Remember to keep holy on the Sabbath," Oliver had some difficulties. He never went to church. But keeping the third commandment was a problem for a different reason: Oliver couldn't be holy just on the Sabbath, because he was holy all seven days of the week, every week of the year.

There was one commandment in which he excelled: the fourth. He honored his mother and father, and he did it in a unique way. We usually think that people bring honor to their parents by their accomplishments. Parents take pride in the success of their children: a graduation, an award, financial success, worldly honors. So much to do with honor is filled with the pride of life. Oliver gave honor to his parents in a different way. He honored them by revealing them to us. We learned from him what kind of people Catherine and José are.

And now it is over. A love story, thirty-three years in the

making. Now the de Vinck family has an angel in paradise to look after them.

Oliver's four-year-old nephew, Danny, in Pennsylvania, reacted to the news of Oliver's death by going from door to door in his neighborhood happily explaining to everyone that his uncle died, and now he can walk.

His nephew, Gregory, went a step further when he said, "Now Oliver can fly, can't he?"

Yes he can. Oliver is free at last, free from the confinement of his own body. He now has all eternity to laugh and dance and yes, fly about in the fullness of life. This is truly a day of celebration. Let us rejoice and be glad.

Chapter XIII

Oliver was out to set things in order perhaps. What I have discovered is that he reveals who *we* are. We look into the eyes of the other and we see ourselves. Each person is a universe, or a dynasty. The world we live in today seems to ignore this. The individual has become the consumer. Our values are determined by television scripts and by what is in vogue. Haven't we become a nation of people afraid to speak of innocence and softness? Aren't we concerned today with being right and being better than our neighbors? What gods do we honor? We are tricked into wearing certain clothes, fooled into buying dazzling machines, duped into voting for a man or woman who lacks substance.

Our world is trying to bend reality, reshape itself into the most amount of comfort and profit.

When my son, David, was three years old, I began to teach him the idea that everything has an inside. We split apples in half, peeled open tight spring buds; listened to our heartbeats with a toy stethoscope.

I began to think about the inner nature of things when I first read about a New England tradition. I must have been ten or eleven. "After a barn is complete, the builders place coins on each beam for luck."

I lived in a house that was built in 1900. Perhaps there is something on the exposed beams down the basement, I thought. I took my imagination and hope to the dark rooms of the furnace and washing machine and spent the afternoon standing on a chair and passing my hand over dust and soot until I hit something thin and hard about the size of a piece of typing paper. When I brought it down to my lap, I rubbed away the dirt. "N.J." and "09" were printed to the far right in bold white letters; to the left, the numbers 972. I had discovered a genuine 1909 New Jersey license plate made with iron and enamel by the Horace E. Fine Auto Tags Company in Trenton, N.J. (so stamped on the reverse side). It was one of the greatest objects I found as a child.

The archaeologist understands the quest for a hidden reality, as does the poet. I believe, however, that we, the American public, are quickly losing our ability to see this hidden reality.

We have advertising agencies that manipulate words to convey misleading information and images. We have educational policies based on political truths and ambitions. We have political campaigns created by speech writers, television directors, and polltakers. Government is deceiving government. We have a floundering foreign policy sewn together with the needles of nuclear weapons.

As Sir James Frazer observed in his book *The Golden Bough,* ancient people believed the world was animate, that every natural object, trees and plants and animals, had its spirits, or to speak more properly, its shadows.

Haven't we sneered at such innocence without science and convictions? Haven't we reshuffled the center of the universe away from those spirits and redirected our Western eyes toward all that is visible and immediate and comfortable?

At a recent wedding I attended, all the unwed girls stood behind the bride as she blindly tossed the bouquet over her shoulder. Each young woman took a quick step backward, and let the flowers drop to the ground. Everyone laughed.

What is my midsummer night's dream? That my three children dress in transparent gowns and whisper to the trees at midnight; that my two little Mad Hatters and my little girl exchange stories about wild things and giant peaches.

Are we becoming a godless people, doubting more and more the inner existence of spirits and the immeasurable consequences of hope and compassion? Do you doubt the inner existence of Oliver?

If our leaders persist in forming judgments based on collective indecisions and revisions solely out of fear and to protect public ratings, soon enough there will be a cry, "But the king has no clothes!"

If we persist in the conscious efforts of misleading people simply because we want their dollars, we will depend more and more on avarice to maintain our economy.

If we devise more and more refined methods to re-create life; if we devise more and more refined methods and reasons to create death, we run the risk of ignoring the primitive, innocent, and mysterious insides of who we are.

In the advent of each presidential election I ask, where are the men and women who pay homage to deeper truths? Even my eight-year-old son knows that everything has an inside.

Can a man or woman of wisdom and compassion stand up in our self-centered, superficial world and say, "Enough. Let us return to the shadows. Let us not allow the flowers to fall upon the ground."

My mother told me that during her labor, before I was born, she remembers seeing white bits of piecrust in the crevices of her fingernails. She had been baking a peach pie that afternoon.

This is always my first thought when someone asks me on a form, "Where were you born?" I often wish to answer, "Good Samaritan Hospital, Suffern, New York, 1951, August third. There was, at home, a peach pie on the kitchen table."

We are born into a particular place, by chance, where objects are already arranged in order: neighborhood, doors, carpets, porcelain. We can never change the facts of our own personal history, but it seems to me that the older I get, the more the world attempts to alter the colors and sentiments of what I remember.

As I was driving to work one morning, I stopped at the only traffic light of my commute. While I waited for the light to change green, I looked at my gas gauge, at the taillights of the car ahead of me, at the houses to my left: a green one, a blue one, and then I saw Roe's obstetrician.

I was surprised to see this kind good man standing on the lawn of what was, surely, his home. I hadn't seen him since our last child, Michael, was born ten months before, and there he was, the doctor. His hands were on his waist. He was surveying the new aluminum siding which was being installed against the weathered clapboards. I watched him step cautiously among the loose debris that the workmen had left strewn on the grass, watched him tilt his head back as he admired the new look to his Dutch colonial. And I was sad.

This doctor, this man was the first person to touch all my children. He cupped his hands around the heads of David, Karen, and Michael as they were all born two and three years apart.

I've paid my bills to the doctor; Roe went for her six-month checkup. All is well, but seeing that man again, on his lawn, made me wish I could step out of the car and show him pictures, thank him, invite him home. I wanted to tell him that David is beginning to read, and that Karen just learned to pull on her own socks. I wanted to tell him that Michael looks like his brother, and that he took his first step last week. I wanted to tell the doctor these things, but our world doesn't want such continuity anymore. Our world doesn't want a community anymore. We go from person to person with our dollar bills and credit cards, buy goods and services, and then we go home and close the doors behind us.

I still carry with me the doctor's smile when my first son was born. I still remember how this man wheeled Roe to the recovery room and gently wiped her forehead with a cool damp cloth. I remember the color of his hair, the wrinkles around his eyes. These things I keep with me, but the memories match less and less the man I saw on the lawn that morning.

I try to preserve the past. I take photographs, return to books I once loved. I gather souvenirs.

Four months after Roe and I were married, I moved out of the house where I had lived all my life. In October of 1977, after we packed our clothes and furniture, my desk and books into the orange U-Haul truck, just before we were to leave, I walked alone behind the house. I stopped at the trash can, lifted the lid, and looked inside. A squashed cereal box, magazines, eggshells; then I found what I was looking for—a clean container, a Pringles Potato Chips canister.

I placed the canister under my arms, then I walked through the yard where my brothers and I jousted with lily stems in the spring when we were young, the yard where my grandmother sat in the sun with her shoes beside the chair as she read the newspaper.

I walked to the apple tree which provided us with years of applesauce and apple fights, the tree good for climbing and giving a boy a place to survey and control the world from up between the green leaves and blossoms.

I stood at the base of the tree and scooped a fresh layer of soil into the potato chip can. I walked back to the driveway and placed the canister into the U-Haul, then Roe and I drove down the driveway and into our future.

The doctor's house is now completely encased in aluminum; the hospital where my children were born has been converted into condominiums, but I still have my bit of soil in the box on my shelf, and I like the smell of peach pie.

Chapter XIV

Dear Sir:

I am writing this letter to thank you for your editorial on April 10th concerning "The Power of the Powerless." It is not often that one sees a newspaper of such prominence as *The Wall Street Journal* print an article of that nature. Value is an elusive entity. It, in a sense, defies definition. Yet, we in our humanness attempt to place value on time, resources and even on life. We attempt to measure the quality of life, and the value of one's life, by a standard that, at best, is arbitrary, capricious and self-serving.

The article affected me in a personal way because I have grown up with a brother with Down's Syndrome, or in

cruder terms, he is a mongoloid. The joy and love and
happiness he has brought into my life is beyond descrip-
tion. Sure, there were times of embarrassment, like when
you are in a crowded grocery store and he breaks into an
uncontrolled laughing fit. Yet, through all of the discom-
fort, I learned the greatest lesson that life can teach, and
that is how to love and be loved.

In our society it is so easy to measure everything in dollars
and cents, profits and losses. Yet, we must understand that
much of life challenges these narrow descriptions. Value,
such as the value of the human life, in an ultimate sense,
cannot be measured by self-interested, self-serving, capricious standards. The "powerless" have much to offer us as
a society if we are willing to rethink our narrow ideals of
value and of worth.

> Thank you,
> Dan Hamann
> Seattle, Washington

New Mexico. Virginia. Florida. Colorado. Illinois. Nebraska.
Delaware. New York. Texas. Ohio. New Jersey. Massachusetts.
Wisconsin. Washington. California. Alabama. I received letters
from people all over the country after they read about Oliver.

I believe there is in the heart of our nation, which was built
upon freedom and compassion, a desire to help others. The problem is too often people do not know how to turn that desire into
action. The Peace Corps is certainly an attempt. The Special
Olympics is living proof that if you give people the opportunity
to reach out and help, people will reach out.

Couldn't we establish a national program where we all take on
the responsibility of caring for the world's Olivers? What if a
college decided to include in their core curriculum a require-
ment that a student must take care of an Oliver for a day and give

the mother and father time to go to dinner? What if a corporation allowed each of their employees one day off a year to tend to a child like Anthony? Why do we spend so much of our national conversation defending our personal right to comfort? Let us talk about suffering. Let us talk about the mysteries hidden inside the unborn child which will be revealed to us if we just take the courage to believe in the possibilities.

Vince and Angie took their son home to see what would happen. Peter and his wife understand that their daughter Lauren made a difference in the world.

"But," my parents replied, "he is our son. We will take Oliver home, of course." The good doctor answered, "Then take him home and love him."

Dan Hamann of Seattle, Washington, discovered what his brother had to reveal. My flight to the West Coast was to be the last on my journey as I tried to see what lingered long after Oliver's death. I dipped my hands in the Pacific Ocean, flew over Mt. Rainier, and I sat quietly in a chair and listened to Dan speak about the power of his powerless brother, Paul.

*   *   *

When Paul was born thirty-five years ago, Down's Syndrome was still completely unknown. The doctors said to my father, "You have a Down's Syndrome child and we can't tell you much beyond that."

The whole beginning of everything for my parents was very painful. Paul was born in Seattle. At that time they were putting all women out when they were to deliver their babies, so my mother didn't know what was going on, and my dad wasn't allowed in the delivery room.

Paul was born at about three o'clock in the afternoon, and the doctor came out to my father and said, "Congratulations, Mr. Hamann. You have a healthy, bouncing baby boy."

Everyone went about doing their work. Everyone was ecstatic.

My mom was twenty-one and my dad was twenty-one. It was their first child. Dad had just gotten out of Bible school. He had just been appointed to his first church so he was all excited.

My dad comes from a pretty well-to-do family from Chicago. My grandfather worked for AT & T until he retired at sixty-five, then he moved to Florida. Here was my father, the world ahead of him with a new wife. They had been married less than a year. My mom got pregnant three weeks after their wedding day.

The first words about Paul were, "You've got a healthy, wonderful son," so my father went home to let both mother and baby rest.

The next morning he got a phone call from another doctor.

"Mr. Hamann. I have some bad news to tell you. Your son has Down's Syndrome."

My dad had no idea what that was. He had never heard the term before.

"Well, what does that mean?"

"Your son is mentally retarded. He is severely retarded. What I suggest to you is that you leave the child here, that you don't see it, don't go near it. Don't do anything. Don't tell your wife right away. You'll have to tell her, but don't tell her right away. Don't allow your wife to see the baby, and just leave it here. Everything will be wonderful."

My dad was twenty-one. His folks were out in Chicago. He didn't know what he was going to do. He was shocked. It just blew his whole world right there in that very moment.

He went from euphoria, "I've got a healthy baby son," to shock all in the span of one day.

My mom kept asking for Paul, her new son. She kept asking for him, and the nurses kept saying, "Well, he's real small so we have to keep him in the incubator." My mom hadn't seen Paul yet. She started to sense something was wrong. It was the next day, and still she was asking for him.

"I couldn't tell her," my father said. "I didn't know how to tell her. I didn't know what to say." So he got the president of the Bible school that he had gone to. The president was a very close friend of our family: Charles Butterfield. He was a wonderful older man. He looked like Albert Einstein with the gray hair and the bushy eyebrows.

Mr. Butterfield, his wife and my father went to the hospital where my mother was staying.

"I'll never forget that day," my father said, "that day we told her."

They walked inside the room. A nurse wheeled my mother's roommate out.

"I knew something was happening," my mother told me years later. "I saw your father come in with the Butterfields. I was wondering what was going on."

My dad couldn't tell her. He couldn't get it out. That's not like him. He's a communicator. He just couldn't talk. He just didn't know what to say.

The Butterfields quietly stepped up to my mother, and Mrs. Butterfield then with as much peace as she could manage told my mother.

"I'll never forget," my father said, "because your mother screamed a long sustaining cry. I'll never forget that, hearing your mother scream."

She didn't see Paul for five days after that, and then she went home. It was a total of nine days before my mother saw and held her firstborn child.

My dad was going through all these changes. He didn't know what to do. It was just a horrible, horrible thing. Paul was horribly malformed.

"I didn't know what to do, or what to say. I couldn't believe this was true. But I really knew what to do, really. He was my son. We were going to keep him. After a month we got our heads together and finally brought Paul home."

My dad started to cry when he told me about my mom screaming. I could tell that the sound was still echoing in his mind.

So Paul came home. That was his start.

It's funny growing up. I remember my grandmother. We were
in Florida for a visit. I was probably thirteen and my grandmother was blaming my mom for Paul. "Well, it couldn't have
been Jim's fault. It had to be your fault, Phyllis, because I know
my son would never have a Down's Syndrome baby."

About ten years ago I was sitting in the living room with my
dad. He and I were watching this movie on television. It was
about this woman who had this baby, and they told the woman at
the hospital that the baby died. The woman had given birth a few
hours before. The woman kept having this dream when she came
home that the baby was still alive.

We were watching this film, my father and I.

Finally, at the end of the show, it turned out that this nurse was
in the black market. She was stealing babies and selling them for
lots of money. It ended up that the mother eventually found her
baby.

It was real touching. I looked over and I noticed that my dad
was crying. I tried to figure out why. The show was good, but it
wasn't that good. I sat down beside him and asked, "Dad. What's
going on?"

"Well, you know, I've always wondered if something like that
ever happened with Paul, because when he was first born I saw
him. There are always signs about Down's Syndrome children,
their hands, their eyes, but the doctor said right away that I had a
healthy, normal son."

Then my father walked upstairs and returned with this piece
of paper. On this paper was a list of all the baby boys who were
born in the hospital on the day of Paul's birth.

"I've had this paper for twenty-five years. I've always wondered. For years I thought I was going to go and look up all these
boys and just go see. I wasn't going to talk to them. I wasn't going

to do anything. I was just going to see if there was some six-foot seven young man running around with prematurely gray hair. If one of those young men on that list looked a little like you or me. I've always wondered if something like that was possible. It was always in me. I've kept these names for twenty-five years. I've kept this piece of paper. I'm not going to do anything now, but it has always been in the back of my mind. It doesn't matter. It never mattered because Paul is our son. We raised him. He will always be my son, but always in the back of my mind I've wondered if there is another Jim Hamann running around somewhere."

They brought Paul home. There was no treatment for a child with Down's Syndrome at the time. My parents tried everything to get some treatment for Paul, but it was like, "Your child is going to be nothing, so there is nothing we can do."

Paul didn't walk until he was three. My mom carried him around until he was three.

Right after my mom had Paul, she and the baby went to a church meeting. All the people they had been in Bible school with were there. There were a lot of other women there. Three or four of my mother's friends had had babies at the same time. They were all sitting there nursing their babies. Mom was holding Paul.

"I remember," my mother said, "I remember all the women coming in to all my friends and saying, 'Oh what a lovely baby you have.' I sat there all by myself. No one ever said a word to me. I remember sitting there thinking that Paul was so ugly."

As the story unfolded, my parents discovered that many people didn't know what to say; doctors didn't know what to do. It was horrible for my parents. Paul didn't walk. My mom was told that she could never have any more children because she had tumors. It was really a miracle that my older sister and I came along.

Paul, when he was three, pulled a lamp over on top of himself and cut his eye, cheek, all the way down his face. They thought he was going to die. He still has a big scar across his eye.

Paul had to wear diapers always, but my mom took him around with her anyway. My father said that he had a hard time in the beginning. "I really couldn't take Paul anywhere because I had so much pride. I had a hard time taking him out. Your mother never had an ounce of trouble with that."

"That's right," my mother said. "He's my boy and I don't care what people think. I come from a small town in Idaho. Paul is my son."

But my father had a difficult time with it. My whole family had a hard time with it. Paul was a real complication for the perfect scenario. He was unplanned. It was hard for my dad to adjust to it.

If I were to think of it from a philosophical or theological perspective, I'd say that is the reason the Lord decided for us to have Paul, really for my dad.

My father says it to this day. "I know it. Paul came into my life for me."

I can say the same thing for myself. My family, we are strong. We're demanding. We're the typical leader types, and sometimes we lose touch with people, with feelings and emotions. We get separated from the hurt.

Paul has opened up a world, a new world for me and my father. That world might never have been opened. I, like my father, could have been a shallow, hard, demanding, domineering person. We could have been impervious to people's hurts and pains, but Paul brought a dimension into my father's life, into my life, which has given us an extraordinary balance.

It would be like the Kennedy family. They've had so much hurt in their lives which must have brought them some balance to the excitement and vigor and strength they possess.

The Lord used Paul to bring balance into my father's life, to make him the good man he is. He is warm and so giving to people, so compassionate. People love my father. He is still a Hamann, six-foot five, stern, the leader. He's got the hand on the helm of the ship. He's got vision and direction. He's going somewhere, yet at the same time he is accessible, and he's caring, and he's warm, and I *know* Paul unlocked many of those things in my father, and in me too. There is a need to be unlocked. We all need to be unlocked. It is a question of who has the key. Paul had the key.

My sister, Lori, was born nine years later, and I was born a little over a year after that. My mother had three children in diapers when Paul was twelve. That is when things became seriously difficult.

Paul was just beginning to enter his adolescence. As the new hormones set in, as he began to grow, as new things began to stir inside Paul, he moved from being this sweet, docile, complaisant child to an angry, jealous stranger.

Paul couldn't communicate. He couldn't say anything, and he was physically strong. He is not large, but he is strong.

He couldn't speak because no one knew how to teach him how. All he did was grunt. He still hadn't been to a school a day in his life.

When Lori and I came along he was in touch with the notion that mom's and dad's affections were being divided among the children and not reserved for him exclusively. The new adolescent. The new hormones pumping through his body. Paul became violent. He was just out of control.

My parents could not leave Paul alone in a room with me or with my sister because he would go after us. He tried to choke me several times.

Once, when I was about ten years old, Paul pulled the T.V. down on top of me because he couldn't cope with all the things that were going on around him. It got to the point where it was just impossible for my parents because they could not watch us all at the same time.

My mother said that she had to install a lock on the outside of Paul's door. She was trying to regulate this thing. She told me about the time she was out in the yard gardening when she just got this feeling that there was something wrong. She remembered locking Paul's door, but she got this feeling just the same. We were all supposed to be down for naps.

She came into the house and there was Paul—he had me down on the floor. He had my face pressed into the big high shag carpet in the living room. I was blue. I was almost dead. He was smothering me. He didn't realize what he was doing, but he was doing it.

My mother threw Paul off me as I was gasping for breath.

There were a series of circumstances like that. My parents were at a complete loss about what to do.

It came to the day when Paul had taken Lori. We were all outside. My mother stepped inside the house for a moment. She had just walked through the door when Paul threw Lori, who was four and a half at the time; he threw her onto the ground, took her by the head. He began pounding and pounding her head onto the rocks. He split her head open.

My mother rushed outside and rushed Lori to the hospital. My sister was O.K., but that was the last straw.

I remember the day that they drove Paul to the institution. It was ripping my parents apart. It was tearing my mother in two. She loved Paul. She loved Lori and me, but she just didn't see how it could possibly work.

The state institution at that time was a hell. It was terrible. I remember the pattern of our lives at that time.

Paul would come home every weekend, and every Saturday night, late, we would drive him back to the institution. I remember sitting in the car. I hated that place. I hated it. It was like an army compound with huge army barracks. We drove through these high guarded gates. The low dark buildings were called dorms where four boys lived in each. Dorms.

I remember driving there every Saturday night. The buildings were run-down. We drove into the compound and pulled up to Paul's barrack.

I remember as a child my dad turning to us saying, "Lock the doors," and we'd lock the car doors.

Paul would step out. The retarded people milled around in the darkness. I remember retarded men lumbering up to the car and banging on the windows. I was eight. They pressed their faces against the windows. They punched the windows and did funny things: drool, lick the glass, squash their noses flat.

My mother cried every Saturday night as we drove Paul back. My dad would take Paul out of the car and return him into this hellhole. There were ninety or one hundred guys and maybe three adults. They had slop for food. I remember going into Paul's room. There were cots, just cots. No tables or lamps.

Saturday night was bath night. We'd come and there would always be all these naked men doing these crazy things. I didn't know how to interpret that.

I'll never forget driving there one day. We drove up and there was a man sitting on the ground eating dirt. I remember the dirt coming out of his mouth. I remember saying, "Mommy. Mommy. Why is that man eating dirt?"

"Honey, he's like your brother. He doesn't know."

"Well, why doesn't somebody stop him?"

"Well," she said, "they probably don't know that he's doing that."

"I want to go out and stop him."

"You can't do that," she insisted. "You can't do that." She wouldn't allow us out of the car.

Paul lost all but two of his teeth while he was there.

We went through that every Saturday night for as long as I can remember. About ten years ago something changed. I don't know what it was. Was it funding? Attitudes changed? They tore all the barracks down and built new apartment complexes, and there's been a progression of increased care over the last few years. Paul started school. It is different now than it was. Paul has his own room. There are five people in an apartment complex and one trained professional. They have their own eating facilities. It is all just done lovely. Things have changed, but remembering back how horrible it was, I can never quite separate the two. I still drive in to that institution, and I still get that knot in my stomach. I remember how it was.

My parents still continue to struggle with Paul. Looking back I see that I too had my struggle. When Paul would be home on weekends, we often took him to the store where he would get into one of his uncontrollable laughing fits. He would laugh, and I would run. If we were in the grocery store, I'd run to the next aisle so people wouldn't think that I was with him.

I remember thinking as I was growing up, What am I going to say to my friends?

I remember going into junior high school. People would always say, "Are you the youngest?" and I'd always say yes. "I have an older sister." Often they'd ask if there were any other kids and again I'd say yes. "I have an older brother." Then I would hope that they would not ask the next question because I would not know how to answer it.

"Well, where is he?"

"Well, he's got Down's Syndrome, and he doesn't live at home right now."

I would get funny stares. "My brother is mentally retarded."

People would bring it up in conversation and say, "Oh yeah, you have an older brother. What does he do for a living?" What could I say? It was always that way, so I tried to avoid it as much as I could. Then something happened.

I was in seventh grade, just starting my teens. I went to one of our junior football games. I went to watch the game and to be with my friends. My parents decided to come along, and they brought Paul. I remember sitting next to him on the stands. All my friends were there. This was the first major exposure that my friends had to my family and to Paul.

We were the perfect family with the suburban home, two cars, a picket fence. We went to a private school. We had money, and then there was Paul. I didn't really know how to relate to that. All my friends were very affluent, even more affluent than we were. Paul was a complication.

Even through junior high I was still struggling with trying to make Paul a part of my life. I was trying not to be ashamed of him. I was going through all the identity things that kids go through at that age. I was trying to fit in. I was trying to be one of the guys. I was trying to do all the things the other guys were doing. I just wanted to be accepted. I just wanted to be normal. Yes, I was pretty good in sports, and that helped me, but here I was. I just wanted to be one of the guys, and I had Paul.

My parents brought Paul to the football game. I sat next to him. Then, I can't say why, I started walking him around the field a little. I held his hand. I don't know if it was instantaneous or if it was something in me, I suddenly got proud of Paul.

I sat down next to him again. I still held his hand, then I walked him around again, and I introduced all my friends to him. From that moment on I was changed. I don't know how it happened, or why it happened. Maybe, suddenly, I grew up. I don't know what happened.

I loved Paul. I always loved Paul. He has always shown his love for us. He says, "Danny, Lori, Mommy, Daddy." He says these four words and he says, "bye-bye, hello," and he says, "hi honey," and that's about all. "Danny, Lori, Mommy, Daddy. Bye-bye."

He says things in repetition, "Danny. Danny. Danny. Danny." He says, "Hi Danny. Hi Danny. Hi Danny." He says this over and over again.

Paul is like the rest of us. He likes to be touched. He is warm. He'll reach out and he'll hold and he'll hug. He always wants to hold your hand. I don't know if that is typical of Down's Syndrome people or if it is just Paul.

We have always been very warm. He's always been very warm. It gets to the point where we're sitting in a room and he says my name one hundred and fifty times. "Hi Paul," I say in greeting. In response he goes on and on: "Hi Danny. Hi Danny. Hi Danny. Hi Danny. Hi Danny. Hi Danny." And I say "Hi Paul," each time and he goes on and on, then he reaches out of his chair and hugs me or pats my leg.

I loved Paul. That was never the problem. It was being able to make a transition from shame to proudly acknowledging, "This is my brother." This was hard for me because of all of the things I wanted to be. I wanted to be one of the guys.

It was hard for our whole family. I know mom and dad made a transition long before my sister and I did.

For a long time Paul was the person I loved. Paul Hamann, but not really Paul part of the family Hamann, Paul the brother. Then suddenly at that football game he became my brother.

About a year later I was in school. I happened to witness the beginnings of a fight. One kid came up to the other and they started exchanging words. An argument exploded. One boy shouted to the other, "You stinking mongoloid! You're just a stupid mongoloid!" I remember just standing there. I put my books on the ground, walked up to the name-caller, and I hit him as hard as I could in the face. He was on the ground. I stood over him saying, "You don't know what you're talking about," and I proceeded to fill him in on what a mongoloid was, and that I had a brother who had Down's Syndrome who was a mongoloid, and if I ever heard him say that again I would tear his throat out.

That wasn't really like me. I was a lover, not a fighter, but it just hurt me for him to say that. I watched the situation unfold before me and I had to go in and do something.

Whenever something like that came up, I had to act. For instance, there was a program in our school where they took the mentally handicapped for a swimming session every Tuesday. They would get the people in the water and have them move around. I just had to do something. Every Tuesday morning I'd jump into the water with these handicapped children, and I was proud of it. Somehow I made the transition from Paul being a member of the family to Paul being my brother. Suddenly this whole world opened up to me, a world I had never experienced before.

I remember in high school going to the institution where Paul stayed. There is one section for the most severely deformed people, for the children with the most horrible birth defects. Somehow I was walking through those halls. I saw a lot. It changed me. I started seeing things for the first time that I'd never seen before. As I walked out of the wing I returned to Paul's room. He was sitting on the bed. I walked in, stood there and just cried wondering why things had to be that way, wondering why I had been so selfish and self-centered, and why I had so little love and care and compassion in my heart for just the people around me, let alone for anyone else. Things really changed for Paul and me.

I take Paul out a lot. He and I do things now. I take him to church. I take him to get ice cream cones. We go to basketball games. He doesn't know what the heck is going on at those games, but he likes being with me. I like being with him.

Sometimes he just comes home with me and we watch T.V. together. I have to change his pants when he wets them, and it's all wonderful. It is really odd, but it is all wonderful.

Every time I see someone with a handicap I just cry, just like that. It is not a hurt or pity that I feel, but love, and I can't figure out how come it is that way. Maybe that is the way it is supposed to be. Love. Love for people. Love for life. Love for everything. It has been for me ever since junior high school when Paul became my brother.

The biggest thing that Paul did for me and probably for my

family was that he opened us up to something we would never have experienced otherwise, something about the quality of life that we would have never experienced. He brought us to ourselves.

We are all so connected to our own world. I watched a movie on T.V., *Ordinary People.* A funny thing about that movie is that the mother's life had to be perfect, and when the accident happened, when she lost her son, the mother was not ever able to make the transition. Her life wasn't perfect any longer. Her son died. Things changed forever. Her perfect little world was falling apart, and she was never able to make the transition to accept it and to learn something from it.

I know in my life that Paul represents many things to me: hurt, disunity, disharmony. He represents ugliness. He is not pretty. He represents ugliness in the world. He represents a love with conditions. I loved him within the confines and parameters, and I loved him as long as his ugliness didn't get in the way. I loved him as long as the ugliness of everything that he stood for wasn't part of my life, my real life.

"Yes, I have a brother," I used to say, hoping they didn't ask the next question.

Somehow when I was able to make that transition from recognizing the ugliness to making the ugliness a part of my life, part of my family, part of my love, it opened so many doors. It opened up so many emotions. It opened up everything. Paul has done things for me that I will never be able to explain.

I realize now that Paul was exactly what I needed. I realize that maybe the Pauls and Olivers play that role for all of us. They play the role to connect us to something beyond ourselves. They play the role to maybe personalize some of the things we try to distance ourselves from.

Paul is so warm and so loving and so giving and so kind, and he is so ugly and so perfect at the same time. When he worked himself through the teen years he went back to the old Paul. He is gentle. He's got nothing but good things in his heart. There is no bad in this person. There is no deceit. There is no lying. There is no struggle, no ambition to step on anybody to get to the top. These are all the things that are produced in our society. Paul doesn't have any of those things, yet he is so ugly and so deformed and so inarticulate, and here he is opening up the whole world to me, opening the whole world up to my family and to everybody who touches him.

I wish that somehow more people could experience that. I believe that is why God has allowed Paul and Oliver to exist because they do have a contribution to make. They are a message to us about life. They are a message to us individually. They are a message to people and to the world about life because life is imperfect and life is full of hurt and life is full of pain and ugliness, but we still have to love, and we still have to care, to work our way through it. I know they are here for us.

Paul is in our lives. He is an ambassador sent from the heavenly family to change us forever so that we won't be what we would have otherwise been. I believe that we didn't have the choice which made all this happen to Paul, but we had the choice to make the transition, the transition to life and to love.

Chapter XV

There had been, all my life as a child, an uncompromising embrace for what was good and fanciful and holy. It was the outstretched arms of my mother and father that I followed.

Children dance around the glowing fire if their ancestors teach them how. Oliver was part of that fire: the dry wood, the embers and the mystery in the smoke.

If Oliver had never been born I wouldn't have the same joys and fears and secrets I dream about today. There was a substance in the house of Oliver beyond science and philosophy and theology, for these are man-made explanations. We always feel a need to explain, to touch and hold evidence. We often feel confident that we can make decisions in the present which will guarantee comfortable results in the future. Those guarantees never exist, unless the choices we make embrace the fire in an act of love.

I have regrets and fears, but they are safe in my heart and memory, protecting me as I step among the difficult questions of each day.

Somehow the owl, raspberries and Isabelle all remain with me, those images of delight and fear I return to again and again.

Once, only once, as I was walking home from school along the wide sidewalks, under the maple trees, against the blue crushed stones of the driveway, I came upon a noise above my head, a rustling sound, all feathers and pine needles. I looked up along the trunk of the tree, through the boughs here and there until I saw a Great Horned Owl, wide-eyed and serious, looking directly down at me. I was ten. It was spring. The owl cocked his head to one side. I did too.

My first instinct was to run into the house and tell my mother, "There's an owl! There's a big owl!" My second instinct, which I followed, was to stand still.

"What are you doing there, owl?" I said aloud. Years later I was to read that it was the owl's screech which heralded Caesar's murder. The Romans considered the bird an ill omen. The Talmud says to dream of the owl brings bad luck.

As a ten-year-old, I knew that my owl was something wonderful until he leaped out from his hidden perch, spread open his powerful wings, and rushed over me with purpose. I ran into the house and never told anyone about him.

Children live with secrets and high shadows crossing over them. Living in the house of Oliver heightened, for me, that mystery. We all walk cautiously between our joys and terrors, but we reach out just the same. This all has in my heart something to do with raspberries.

I remember thick, tall raspberry plants which lined the outer edges of my father's woods. I remember the ripe fruit between the green leaves, but I also remember scratching my hands on sharp thorns. I remember popping a raspberry into my mouth and biting into a small beetle. I remember the garter snake passing under my legs. I learned as a child that the best fruit had its price. I remember too the sadness I felt while picking the last two or three berries from the bush in late October, tasting the sweetness one more time before winter. Oliver was like that sweetness.

Who can say what images will stay with us forever and what will be forgotten? Yet somehow they all seem to fit together: owls and raspberries and my brothers and sister; my mother and father and Father John; the diapers, convulsions, the coffin through the window, the laughter, the silence. I tend to agree with the novelist Willa Cather: "Most of the material a writer works with is acquired before the age of fifteen."

When I was a teenager my aunt and uncle from Belgium invited me to spend the holidays with them and with my three cousins: Anne, ten . . . Tessy, twelve . . . and Isabelle, sixteen. We were to travel from Brussels, through Paris, and down to the southern mountains not far from Lascaux and the famous cave paintings.

My grandmother, also from Belgium, paid for my flight and suddenly I was out of the airplane and sitting in a small yellow station wagon with relatives I had never met before.

Anne was a tease; Tessy, a bit of a tomboy, was full of humor and wonderful freckles. But Isabelle, well she was my cousin, but I remember her thick brown hair. She spent most of the two weeks hidden behind a pair of wide sunglasses.

My uncle made all the arrangements. We were to stay in an ancient farmhouse he had rented which had been renovated and cleaned for our arrival. There were two houses, both made of stone. The roofs were covered with moss.

The large house was for my uncle, aunt and for the three girls. The small single-roomed house was for me.

I remember the snails on the rock walls, the poppies, the smell of the mountain air. The farm was well kept, the hay cut, the well clear and deep.

We spent the days touring castles and grottoes. In the evening we read or listened to music on distant stations over the radio my uncle fiddled with which was propped upon the windowsill.

The last night we were to be there we played cards, packed as much as we could for the next day's journey home, ate cheese and fruit. Then, too quickly, it was time for sleep. I crossed the small courtyard which separated the two houses, stepped into my little cottage, locked the door behind me, and then I went to bed.

Somewhere in the middle of the night I heard a slight knocking at my closed window shutter. I remember lying in bed, pressing the darkness from my eyes. I knew I was in the middle of France, in the middle of an isolated farm. I didn't know that I was between that great excitement and fear which teaches us to remember.

The tapping was repeated and I pulled the covers from my bed and stepped to the closed window.

"Christopher," I heard someone whisper outside. "Christopher."

I unhooked the latch and slowly pushed open the thick wood shutters like open arms outstretched, and there in the moonlight was Isabelle in her long white nightgown.

"Would you like to come and dance in the meadow with me?"

"What?" I asked in my tattersall pajamas and bare feet.

"Would you like to come dance in the meadow?"

"Oh no," I said as I closed the shutters and went back to bed.

We all have regrets usually kept back in our youth like secrets which become more and more sweet as we grow older.

I dream of the owl and of Oliver and of the taste of my father's raspberries. I wish I had danced with Isabelle under that safe and frightening moon.

Chapter
XVI

Because Sargent Shriver read about Oliver that day in *The Wall Street Journal*, I was invited to Washington to meet him, to meet his wife, Eunice Kennedy-Shriver, and to meet the people who give life and love to the Joseph P. Kennedy, Jr. Foundation which was established in 1946 by Ambassador and Mrs. Joseph P. Kennedy in honor of their eldest son who was killed in World War II. Since its inception, the foundation has initiated and stimulated programs of scientific research, training, service, education and sports in the area of mental retardation.

Because of Oliver I was invited to turn my pen toward the cause of the Special Olympics. I was asked by the Kennedy Foundation if I might be able to write a few things in preparation for their fortieth anniversary celebration. I was honored, flattered, intimidated. Oliver led me to splendid places and to splendid people.

I wrote the foundation a poem, judged a competition, and prepared these words:

On August 12, 1944, Joseph P. Kennedy, Jr., was killed in an attempted bombing mission in Europe. The Kennedy family did not realize at the time that this event would pose a question for them, a question some of us come to when we are very young. Some of us ask this question when we are very old. Some of us never ask: Why suffering?

We can all look back to our lives and embrace, again, those moments when we lost faith, or love, when we questioned the absurdity of life and raged at the dying of the light in Dylan Thomas' words.

Joseph Kennedy, Sr., lost his oldest son to the Second World War. There is little need to describe his grief, for this same grief rests in all of us. Who among us has not endured the sudden anguish of losing a brother or sister, mother or father?

President Kennedy was right when he wrote that, "Joseph's worldly success was so assured and inevitable that his death seemed to cut into the natural order of things."

Of course it was this very natural order of things which the Kennedy family had to confront for the first time.

What I ask of you is to consider what can rise from the flames of the burning phoenix.

How did you fill the sudden void once grief lost its potency? On August 12, 1946, the second anniversary of Joseph's death, Mr. and Mrs. Kennedy established the Joseph P. Kennedy, Jr. Foundation. The Kennedy family chose to create a new life from the dark ashes of their grief.

There is an alchemy in sorrow, as Pearl Buck reminded us. It can be transmuted into wisdom.

Through the alchemy of sorrow which the death of the oldest son represented to the Kennedys, a new element was added to our social conscience concerning the handicapped and the mentally retarded.

For many years there existed a suspicion and shame attached to the birth of a child whose head was unusually large, or whose spine was twisted. There was a fear of a child who was born with aberrant brain functions. There was a tendency in our society to encourage parents to push such a child aside. There was a social attitude that believed such a child was, simply, a mistake. Mothers and fathers didn't believe this, but we as a country and a people did. We are quick to pursue our own comforts.

The Joseph P. Kennedy Foundation offered one of the first voices in the history of the United States which asked, "What are these children trying to tell us?"

Because of the Kennedy Foundation, scientific research was given a new focus. Community centers were created, legislation was passed, scholarships were granted . . . all to investigate and support the mysteries the mentally handicapped embrace.

Because of the new awareness, many of us have allowed ourselves to join the community of suffering.

The Joseph P. Kennedy Foundation was established forty years ago to understand the phenomenon of life.

I can think of nothing better which celebrates this life than the foundation's Special Olympics. I quote one of thousands of letters the Special Olympics receives:

> I would like to share a story with you about a boy named John. He is my son, and he is special. I am proud of him and of his accomplishments which came as a result of his being in the Special Olympics. They are such caring, helpful people who spurred John into doing things that we thought were never possible. John joined Special Olympics when he was about ten years old. They taught him

how to run a race and come out a winner. This gave him courage and pride in himself. Even when he didn't win, they congratulated him for trying, and gave him courage to try again.

Through the years he has learned to play basketball and baseball. He can now do the running broad jump and he can bowl and ski.

John also learned at the Special Olympics how to get along with other special athletes. They always encourage each other and give each other a sense of worth. The older ones help the younger ones.

As a result of all this training, encouragement, love and understanding, John has grown into a self-reliant young man. He had the courage and confidence to go out into the real world and get a full-time job. He has held this job for over six months now, and we feel this would not have been possible without his experience in the Special Olympics.

Because Joseph P. Kennedy, Jr., died in a fiery crash over England forty years ago, a foundation was created which taught this young Special Olympian courage and confidence.

We cannot create significant advantages for ourselves. We cannot try and outguess the future. We can, simply, contribute to that phenomenon of life by choosing to establish patterns and habits which sustain life.

Instead of giving into grief, Joseph's parents allowed the memory of their son to rise and reach out into the present and help someone to learn confidence and courage.

With the growing social awareness that the mentally retarded might just be a cornerstone of our community, President John F. Kennedy signed into law P.L. 88-164 on October 31, 1963, and created the President's Committee on Mental Retardation. This established funds for twelve mental retardation research centers throughout the country.

Long before its actual structure had been studied, it was believed that man's inner nature was reflected in the hand. Today we know that his inner nature is reflected in the brain. Mental retardation is not a curse from the gods; it is not a supernatural phenomenon, or something to fear.

Because President Kennedy signed into law P.L. 88-164, we know more about what mental retardation is than we have ever known. Simply, President Kennedy encouraged neuroscientists to focus on brain development and how such development is related to the mentally retarded. We have come to realize that we can accomplish more if we can understand the function of each child's brain.

Scientific research for the mentally retarded is vast and complex. We know much, but there is a full one third which we know absolutely nothing about. It is because science was brought to focus its attention on aberrant brain function, however, that we have learned so much in the last twenty-five years.

It was P.L. 88-164 and the Kennedy Foundation which allowed research scientists the time to identify normal sequences of structure and functional growth of the brain so that they were able to compare these findings to abnormal brain development. The scientific community needed to know what it took to form a normal cerebral cortex. Once this standard was established, scientists could begin to investigate developments which were not normal.

Before President Kennedy's initiative, science was groping for a language to define abnormal functions basic to what mental retardation is.

The research centers established by President Kennedy's signature allowed for multidisciplinary research in aberrant human development. Scientists must come together at research centers and work together. This is not the age for private ambitions.

The President's Committee on Mental Retardation reminds us that medicine is not a health profession, but a helping profession.

We really cannot let go. That is the quest. It is a quest for certainty and if we are open-minded about it, we know that we will never be certain, but we know from what we have seen in the past history of the Kennedy Foundation that there is a gratitude for receiving, but there is a greater gratitude for giving.

I recently asked a father of a Down's Syndrome child to speak about his son's place in this world of ours.

> For so many years people gave up on kids like my son Kyle. They put them in an institution, or hid them somewhere.
>
> If you give any kid a chance, he will grow. My son has personality. He does things. Give a kid like Kyle a chance, and he can learn to live up to his potential.
>
> When Kyle was born, my mother couldn't even bear to look at him. My parents were hard and intolerant of people if they were not just like themselves. They used to stare at someone who was retarded, or laugh.
>
> Today Kyle loves to go to his grandparents' house. He has this routine. My father makes him popcorn, and then he sits in this certain chair. Kyle sits there with his popcorn.
>
> When Kyle was born my mother couldn't look at his deformed ears, his slanted eyes, the scar on his chest from the heart operation. When my wife and I were showing her the exercises we were doing with Kyle, my mother could not even look at him. She wanted nothing to do with it. She just couldn't stand it.
>
> Today my mother is the first one to give Kyle a bath and splash water all over him. Kyle has changed her life.

It is for Kyle and his family that the Kennedy Foundation was created. It is for Kyle and his family that President Kennedy signed Public Law 88-164.

Today I see and hear all around me a cold maturity and toughness. I hear people speak about the quality of life, expediency, instant pleasure, the quick destruction of suffering and pain—instant solutions.

Let us not lose confidence in ourselves and in our past dreams. Let us not give a false structure to what is in our own hearts.

Let us not be the Great Gatsby whose dream "was already behind him, somewhere in that vast obscurity beyond the city, where dark fields of the republic rolled on under the night."

Let us be the F. Scott Fitzgerald who believed that "tomorrow we will run faster, stretch out our arms farther."

Let us, as the Gatsby novel concludes, "beat on, boats against the current, borne back ceaselessly into the past."

We, in this country, have a glorious past built on compassion and endurance. We cannot finish our work in our lifetime, but we are also not free to desist from it.

The poet Carl Sandburg concludes his book of poems *The People, Yes* with these words:

> There are men who can't be bought.
> The fireborn are at home in fire.
> The stars make no noise.
> You can't hinder the wind from blowing.
> Time is a great teacher.
> Who can live without hope?

The Kennedy sons were fireborn, rising out of the ashes, creating new life. All parents of a handicapped child know that time is, indeed, a great teacher, and we all know that we cannot live without hope.

We all inherited the earth. Each grain of sand, every shadow belongs to us all.

That is the spirit of the Kennedy Foundation. That is the message President Kennedy's Committee on Mental Retardation brought to all of us, and that is the message I bring to you: We *all* inherited the earth.

Conclusion

After I read Harper Lee's novel, *To Kill a Mockingbird,* when I was fifteen years old, I knew that I wanted to be a father like Atticus. I too wanted to be the type of man who would stay up all night with his son or daughter when he or she was in need.

If you read the book, you will remember how, after Jem, the son, was nearly murdered by Bob Ewell, the villain, a doctor was called to mend the boy's broken arm.

After the doctor left, Atticus "turned out the light and went into Jem's room. He would be there all night, and he would be there when Jem woke up in the morning."

This book spoke to me in ways that I could not understand as a young teenager. I could not know the word "paternal," but I felt, many times while I was growing up, that there was a protective force around me, and that this power somehow, mysteriously, belonged to me too. It was the same power Oliver possessed: that power to protect all that grows around him.

I remember being on vacation in Combermere, Ontario, Canada, with my mother and father. I could not have been more than six years old.

We were visiting Madonna House, the lay apostolate along the Madawaska River, founded by Catherine de Hueck Doherty, a woman in love with God and his poor. My parents were talking in the meeting room, and I, bored with adult conversation, took a walk around the building to see the water.

As I turned the corner, I tripped over my shoelace and gave out a small cry.

"What's that?" someone called out from the back steps.

I quickly stood up and explained to the old man that I had fallen and that my shoe was untied again.

"Come here."

I guessed correctly that the man was Moisë, the old blind Canadian Indian who came to Madonna House for companionship and for a cup of tea.

I walked slowly, cautiously toward him, afraid of his black hat and his crooked eyes.

"Stand next to me. I will tie your shoe."

I remember he smelled of wood and smoke as he slowly bent over and pulled on my lace.

"What's your name?" he asked in a quiet, deep voice.

"Christopher."

That was the entire length of our conversation. He tied my shoe, and then I ran to the river and threw stones and caught frogs for the rest of the afternoon.

Today I still remember good Moisë as he sat on the steps listening to the stones hit the water, and I knew back then that I was safe under his shadow.

Two years later, in the spring, I was to make my first Holy

Communion. I was also to make another discovery about those who invisibly protect us with that power.

For weeks the nuns prepared us with catechisms and rehearsals. I remember kneeling at the wooden altar rail as Sister, pretending she was the host-giving priest, came to each of us and tapped our extended tongues with the closed point of her pen, and then we were supposed to say, "Amen."

At the end of our training, Sister announced we could purchase the Holy Communion packet: a white purse, a white Bible and white rosary beads for the girls; a tie, a black Bible and black rosary beads for the boys.

"Please raise your hand if you'd like to place an order."

I had never, in all my seven years, made a financial decision, so I didn't raise my hand.

On the day of my first communion, after all the rush and fuss, I found myself squeezed inside the church: boys on the left and girls on the right. There was just enough room for the parents in the rear.

The parish priest began the ceremonies with a general blessing, and then he asked all the children to lift their Bibles to be blessed.

I looked around and watched many little white and black Bibles float above my head. I was the only one without a Bible. I felt out of place and lonely.

Then the priest asked that we lift our rosary beads. I would have to endure the pain twice.

Again, everyone did as the priest asked. Just before the blessing was invoked, there was a disturbance at the rear of the church. I turned to look with everyone else. I could not exactly see what was going on except someone was trying to leave his middle seat, squeezing by cramped people. Then I saw it was my father.

He excused himself one more time before stepping out into the aisle.

The ceremony stopped. The priest lowered his hands. The children, one by one, lowered their rosary beads.

My father, with a purpose, walked to the center of the church, reached into his pocket, pulled out his long brown rosary beads, leaned over the pew, stretched his long arm in my direction, handed me his rosary beads, and then he smiled. I smiled too.

He quickly returned to his seat just as the priest announced, with understanding, "Could you *all* please lift your beads for the blessing?"

I lifted my brown rosary beads the highest. I am sure of it.

As the years passed, I began to learn more and more about the subtleties of compassion and guidance.

In 1973 I entered Columbia University for a degree in education. I wanted to teach, which I am still doing, but I also fell into the writing of poetry.

During those new months of my life as a writer, I also stumbled into an English course given by the English department chairman, Professor Karl Kroeber.

He had a beard, which I knew I could never grow. He also had a generous mind and a power I could measure against Atticus and my father and, I hoped, against my own heart.

Because I was charmed by his wit and goodness, I wrote a brief note to Professor Kroeber which included a few young poems, the first ones I wrote really. I simply wished to thank him for a good year.

This is what he wrote in return: "Thanks for your letter. One does benefit from encouragement." Then he went on later to say he liked my poems, and he suggested that I stick to love and nature and to my own writing. That is what I did.

Each writer has in his heart the story of how he began and in his drawer that first legitimate letter of encouragement.

Professor Kroeber and I continue our sporadic correspondence and, maybe without his knowing, his letters of wisdom and encouragement are, for me, protective touchstones.

After I learned all these lessons, Roe gave birth to David one month before Oliver died.

The nurse whisked him from the delivery table and carried him to a traylike machine with dials and lamps which, I was told, was simply to regulate the baby's body temperature.

I walked over and looked at the new crying face. Then I asked the nurse, "Can I touch him?"

"Of course you can touch him," she laughed. "He's your son." And then I held his small leg between my fingers and jiggled him a bit.

How can I guarantee that my boy David will turn a corner someday and meet Moïsë? How will I tell my daughter Karen that I have brown rosary beads in my dresser drawer if she ever needs them? How will I stir the head and heart of my youngest son Michael to write a letter of thanks to his teacher?

I wish to teach my children that someone is always there to protect them invisibly, mysteriously, and that they too will learn the power.

I wish to teach my children that the spirit lingers in us all, past, present and future.

Last autumn David was playing outside with his friends Nicholas, Amy and Claire when he stumbled and fell to the ground. He hit the earth in such a way and with such a force that his left arm became dislocated.

There were the tears, the brave tears, and the rush to the hospital, the X rays, the sling, the exhaustion until, finally, restlessly, David went to sleep in his room with Whiskers and his goldfish popping and ticking the surface water of its bowl.

I sat at the foot of his bed and watched him breathing, then I turned out the light, and I promised myself I would be there when he woke up in the morning.

Two days before Roe gave birth to David, my mother called on the telephone to say that Oliver had a fever. Just a fever. Oliver had had fevers before. Nothing to worry about. That was Sunday,

February 10, 1980. Two days later, on Lincoln's birthday, our first son was born.

My parents came to the hospital to see their new grandchild. They admired David through the thick glass of the nursery. They brought Roe daisies and blue carnations. We all embraced, then my mother said she had to go home because Oliver still had a temperature.

We brought David home, Roe and I. Day by day he drank his mother's milk and breathed and breathed, while my brother was slowly dying of influenza and pneumonia thirty minutes away in the house where I grew up.

Each day my mother called. Oliver's temperature was rising. The doctor came, but there was no change. After the third week my mother called to say that, yes, she knew that Oliver was dying.

On Wednesday, March 12, one month after our son was born, Roe came to the school where I taught to join me for lunch, to show David to my students and colleagues, but she really wanted, above all else, to be with my mother.

After lunch Roe took David and drove to my parents' house which is across the train tracks, five minutes away from school.

Oliver had a terrible last night, gasping for each breath, one at a time. By noon the next day, Oliver was in his mother's arms. She held him. One breath. One breath. "Goodbye, my angel," she said, and Oliver died.

After thirty-two years of tending to him, bathing him, feeding him, "Goodbye, my angel," and she laid his head on the pillow.

My mother walked out of the room, crossed the hall and began to walk down the stairs. That is when Roe entered the house with our new son David, and he was the next human being my mother embraced.

Oliver is buried at the Benedictine Monastery in Weston, Vermont. On his tombstone there it is written, "Blessed are the pure of heart for they shall see God."

"Well, I guess you could call him a vegetable. I called him Oliver, my brother. You would have liked him."

We have the power to sit and nurture all that grows around us. We have the power to give the incubus a name.

I will keep Oliver's red dinner bowl on my shelf. It has been in my hands many times. I know its weight, and I know its depth.

AFTERWORD

Fred Rogers

Chris de Vinck's words reach into that part of me where tears are made, and ever so gently helps me to cry—and to wonder if there isn't a part of each of us which feels powerless and in need of unconditional acceptance.

Oliver and Lauren and Anthony and John and Paul and every other vulnerable human being we may meet reminds us of who we are. I'm grateful that Chris has dared to share what is real to him. I'm grateful that he ". . . ran home . . . took the risk . . . was triumphant."

Not all people are able to accept others—or themselves—in as loving ways as the people in this remarkable book. For those of us who are still trying, the message from the powerless seems clear: "Just be yourself and allow us to help you—in any way you feel we can. Our power comes in simply *being*. Yours can too."